Cliff Richard's
FAVOURITE BIBLE
STORIES

Retold for children by Sue Shaw
Illustrated by John Brennan

CONRAN OCTOPUS

First published in 1993
by Conran Octopus Limited, 37 Shelton Street,
London WC2H 9HN

A CIP catalogue record is available from the British Library

ISBN 1 85029 519 0

Editor *Jane O'Shea*
Editorial assistant *Caroline Davison*
Design *Paul Welti with Alison Fenton*
Production *Jill Macey*

Typeset by The R & B Partnership, England
Printed and bound by Arnoldo Mondadori Editore,
Verona, Italy

Contents

Introduction

WHETHER we're grandparents sitting by the fire reading a book, or little children tucked up in bed listening wide-eyed to our first fairy tale from mum or dad, all of us, no matter what our age, love a good story. Sad or exciting, funny or frightening, there's something about a well told tale that grabs our imagination and won't let go until we reach the end. And with some of the best stories, even when we know the ending, we can revisit them again and again, and find just the same enchantment.

The Bible of course is a book that can be read and understood at all sorts of levels. Those who say it's boring have got it wrong, for surely, at its simplest, it's a book of great and timeless stories – about goodies and baddies, heroes and heroines, battles and adventures, escapes and shipwrecks. Just the sort of stuff to stir the imagination and to provoke a request for more!

What follows, of course, is not the whole Bible. Nothing like it. All I've done is to choose a selection of stories, from both Old and New Testaments, which I think I'd have enjoyed when I was a small kid in India. All of them are good tales in their own right – Joseph and his brothers, for instance, David and Goliath, Jesus stilling the storm. And Sue Shaw, teacher and writer for young children, has done a terrific job in simplifying them, yet retaining all the essential energy and colour. But they're also stories which I hope will hint at something beyond make-believe.

It's no secret that for me the Bible has become a very special book. Certainly it's the only one I read every day, even if it means struggling with just

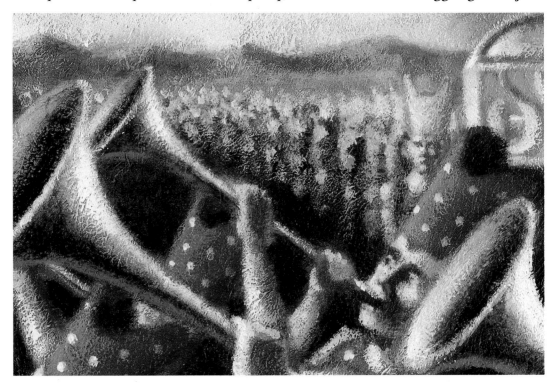

a few sentences before I get to bed late at night! I don't read it through any superstition, nor out of any sort of religious ritual. I read it because I believe that, through it, God teaches me (and anyone else who comes to it with an open mind) about himself and about the sort of person he created me to be. Much of it, of course, is difficult – very difficult – and I doubt if there's anyone, no matter how intelligent or spiritual, who can truly say they understand it all. But, again, that's part of the Bible's mystery – it never seems to give up all its secrets, and can speak to the smallest of children and the wisest of professors.

I guess that, if there is a God who created us, is concerned about us, and even loves us, it's unlikely that he would leave us floundering in the dark. Far more probable that he would give us some means of checking him out and provide some blueprint for life as he intended. Such is the Bible's claim for itself. How he was able to use a variety of writers so long ago, over a great space of time, to communicate his mind coherently is another matter. I, for one, am happy to believe he did!

So, as these Bible stories are told and retold, I pray that they'll have a value far beyond our reckoning. To quote the Bible's own recommended recipe for reading — 'first the milk, then the meat'!

Finally, my thanks to artist John Brennan for such imaginative, powerful and helpful illustrations.

CLIFF RICHARD

God creates the world

*These first stories tell us how God made
the world very wonderful and beautiful but then Adam and Eve spoilt it
because they took no notice of what they were told.*

IN the beginning there was nothing! No noise, no movement, no smells, no places, no people. Nothing. But there was God. And when God spoke, things began to happen.

1. God said, 'Let there be light.' Flash! Bang! There was light. Bright, shining light. God looked at the light and said, 'That's good.'

2. Then God said, 'Let there be sky.' Swish, swish! Suddenly there was sky. Great blue sheets of sky as far as the eye could see and large, white, fluffy rain clouds.

3. Then God said, 'Let there be water and let there be land.' Gurgle, gurgle. Splish, splosh. There was water. Wide, deep seas of water. Rumble, rumble. Crunch, crunch. There was land. Smooth hills, jagged mountains, sandy deserts and curving valleys. And God looked at the seas and the land and said, 'That's good.'

4   Then God said, 'Let there be plants and trees all over the land.'
Heave, heave! Push, push! Up through the soil came trees.

Short, fat, dumpy trees; tall, thin, bendy trees.Then came flowers, soft and silky, smelling sweetly.

And plants, rough and prickly, small and spiky.

There were cherries and chillies, daisies and dahlias.

There were peaches and peppers, beans and beetroot.

5   Then God said, 'Let there be day-time and night-time.' So God made two lights, the sun to shine by day and the moon to shine by night. He also made the stars. Flash! Sparkle! Flash! Sparkle! Thousands and thousands of flickering stars burst into life. And God said, 'That's good.'

Then God said, 'Let there be fish in the seas and birds in the skies.' Whoosh! Splatt! Up came the great whale for a big gulp of fresh air.

Eek! Eek! Out jumped the porpoises, playing in the sunshine. Down in the depths large and small fish wriggled and writhed. There were snappy crabs and sloppy hake, floppy dabs and flabby skate.

High in the sky flew cuckoos and curlews,
Jackdaws and macaws, swallows and sparrows,
Widgeons and pigeons, crakes and drakes,
Swooping and diving, cheeping and squawking.
Then God said, 'Let there be animals.'

All across the land there were wriggly worms and creepy spiders, slimy snails and hissing vipers, smelly skunks and sleepy racoons, cuddly cats and cheeky baboons.

God looked at all he had made and felt really pleased.

'Now I will make people to enjoy the beautiful world I have made,' he said. 'They will be my special friends.'

So God made men and women and he told them, 'I want you to look after this world. Have lots of children and be happy.'

God looked at everything and thought, 'This is VERY good. I have been working hard for six days. The seventh day shall be a day of rest.'

Adam and Eve

WHEN God made the first man, Adam, and the first woman, Eve, they lived in a beautiful place called the Garden of Eden. There were lovely fruit trees, soft, springy grass, sparkling waterfalls and rippling ponds.

'I hope we can stay here for ever,' said Eve.

'We can,' said Adam, 'as long as we remember that God said we can eat from any tree in the garden but not from the good and evil tree.'

But there was a wicked, hissing snake who didn't want their perfect life to last. 'I hate all this happiness. I'm going to spoil it,' he hissed.

One day, when Eve was alone, she heard a swishing sound. It was the wicked, hissing snake.

'You're looking very happy,' he hissed.

'I am. God has given me so much,' she said cheerfully.

'Ah!' the snake sneered. 'But has God given you the good and evil tree?'

'God says we mustn't eat from that tree or we'll die,' Eve replied.

'Oh! That's not really true. You won't die. God's just being mean because he doesn't want you to know everything.'

Eve looked at the good and evil tree and her eyes grew large as saucers.

'Well, it does look pretty,' she thought. 'And maybe God won't really mind.' Eve reached out, took a piece of fruit and ate it.

'I'll give some to Adam, too,' she said. 'It won't do any harm.'

The wicked, hissing snake grinned. Things were about to go very wrong. As soon as Adam and Eve had eaten the fruit they felt guilty and ashamed for the very first time. Then they heard God calling them.

'I'm frightened!' gasped Adam.

'So am I,' cried Eve.

'Quick, let's hide,' said Adam.

They sneaked behind a tree and held their breath.

'Adam! Eve!' called God. 'Are you alright?'

Adam peered out. 'I'm fr-fr-frightened,' he stammered.

'Why?' God asked. 'Have you eaten from the good and evil tree?'

'It's not my fault,' complained Adam. 'You gave me Eve. It's all her fault.'

Eve peered out. 'It's not my fault,' she cried. 'The wicked, hissing snake said you were just being mean and I believed him.'

God felt deeply sad and deeply angry. He shouted at the wicked, hissing snake, 'You horrible, horrible creature. You know very well that now they can't be my friends any more. And they'll grow old and die. You'll pay for this!'

The wicked, hissing snake slithered away, spitting and spluttering.

Adam and Eve felt so ashamed they couldn't even look at God.

'You must go now,' God said sadly.

So Adam and Eve had to leave the beautiful garden and were never allowed back.

Noah and his ark

The Bible is full of very special people who believed
in God and were chosen by him for difficult and sometimes dangerous jobs.
Here you'll meet three of them - Noah, Abraham and Joseph.

MANY years passed. Adam and Eve grew old and died. Their children grew up and had families of their own. Many more years passed. The number of people in the world went on growing. But very few people were friends of God. Most people behaved in wicked and hurtful ways. Except for Noah and his family.

Biff! Boing!

'Ow! Take that!'

Noah looked out of his window. 'Oh no,' he thought, 'another fight!'

'Stop that!' he yelled at the top of his voice.

'Leave us alone!' the men said. 'We like fighting.'

Noah sighed. 'Fighting. That's all people think about. I'm fed up with it.'

Poor Noah! But he wasn't the only one who was fed up with the fighting. God was too.

'I wish I'd never made people,' thought God. 'All they do is hate each other and quarrel. I'm going to send a flood and get rid of them all.'

But first he spoke to Noah.

'You're the only one I can trust,' God said. 'I want you to build a big boat. I'm going to send a lot of rain and there will be a huge flood but you'll be safe if you and your family stay in the ark and do as I say.'

Noah listened, amazed, as God went on:

'When you've finished the boat, fill it with two of every kind of animal and bird.'

'My word!' thought Noah, 'this is going to be a big job!'

Sure enough it took ages to build the boat. Noah's sons, Ham, Shem and Japheth helped him. No-one else did. They thought Noah and his family were stupid.

'Ha! Ha! Noah's gone nutty!' they laughed.

When the boat was finished, Noah filled it with two of every kind of animal and bird, then Noah and his family squeezed themselves into the boat, too.

As God had promised, it began to rain. And rain, and rain, and rain. The waters rose, higher and higher, until all the land was flooded. At last the rain stopped.

Noah looked out. All he could see was water.

'I'll send Mr Raven,' he said, 'to see if there's any land.'

Mr Raven flew out. 'No land, no land,' he cawed.

'I'll send Mrs Dove,' Noah said, but Mrs Dove came back. 'Too wet, too wet,' she cooed.

'My word!' thought Noah, 'this is going to be a long wait!'

Seven days later he sent Mrs Dove out again. This time she came back with an olive leaf in her beak.

'Hurrah!' cried Noah and his family. 'The waters must be going down!'

Seven days later Mrs Dove flew out again but this time she didn't come back.

'Hurrah!' cried Noah and his family. 'It must be safe to leave now!'

Sure enough the land was dry again.

Then God said to Noah, 'It's time to leave.'

'Hurrah!' cried Noah and his family.

So everyone left the boat. The animals came out, two by two, and the birds flew out, two by two.

Then God said to Noah and his family, 'Look after this world. Have lots of children and be happy. And I promise I'll never flood the earth again.'

And God put a rainbow across the sky as a sign to everybody that he would always keep his promise.

Abraham's journey

MANY years after Noah built his ark, there lived a man called Abraham. He was a rich and clever man. God talked to Abraham as he had to Noah, like a friend.

'Abraham,' God said, 'I'm going to make you happy. You will become the father of many people.'

'I've no children,' Abraham thought. 'How can I be a father now?'

'Leave your home and go to the land I will show you,' said God.

It was a terribly hard thing to ask Abraham to do. He had no idea where he was going or how long the journey would be. Still, he packed up and left with his wife, his nephew Lot, Lot's family, their servants and animals and all their belongings. They travelled for many days across the sandy desert until they arrived in the land that God had promised them.

'I will give this land to you and your family,' God said and Abraham believed him.

Time passed. Soon Abraham's servants and Lot's servants began to quarrel.

'Your smelly animals take up too much room,' complained Lot's men.

'And your greedy animals eat all the grass!' protested Abraham's men.

To stop the arguing, Abraham and Lot decided to go to different parts of the promised land.

'You choose where to go,' said Abraham.

'I'll go towards Sodom,' Lot said. So it was agreed.

In Sodom, Lot had many troubles. Four armies attacked Sodom and captured Lot and his family. Lot was scared. He wished he'd stayed with his Uncle Abraham. When Abraham heard Lot had been captured, he rushed off to rescue him. Abraham's men fought long and hard and soon Lot and his family were freed.

Abraham was glad Lot was safe but he felt sad because he still had no child. God knew what Abraham was thinking.

'Don't be frightened,' God said. 'You will have more children than there are stars in the sky.'

Abraham gulped. 'There are an awful lot of stars,' he said, 'but I believe you.'

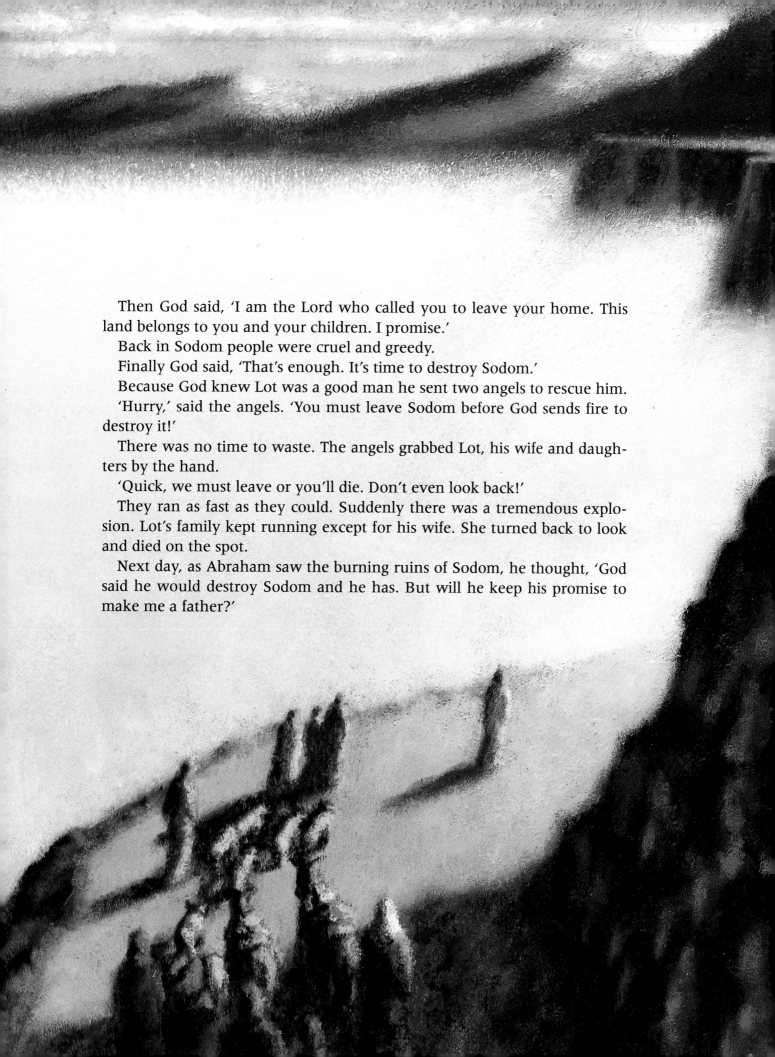

Then God said, 'I am the Lord who called you to leave your home. This land belongs to you and your children. I promise.'

Back in Sodom people were cruel and greedy.

Finally God said, 'That's enough. It's time to destroy Sodom.'

Because God knew Lot was a good man he sent two angels to rescue him.

'Hurry,' said the angels. 'You must leave Sodom before God sends fire to destroy it!'

There was no time to waste. The angels grabbed Lot, his wife and daughters by the hand.

'Quick, we must leave or you'll die. Don't even look back!'

They ran as fast as they could. Suddenly there was a tremendous explosion. Lot's family kept running except for his wife. She turned back to look and died on the spot.

Next day, as Abraham saw the burning ruins of Sodom, he thought, 'God said he would destroy Sodom and he has. But will he keep his promise to make me a father?'

Abraham and Isaac

ABRAHAM became a very old man. In fact he was nearly one hundred years old! He was so old, everyone said:

'Poor Abraham, he'll never have any children now.'

But God had promised Abraham that he would be a father and Abraham believed him. Sarah, Abraham's wife, didn't believe God.

'We're too old for children,' she said. 'God must have forgotten his promise.'

But one day she knew she had been wrong. She was going to have a baby.

When the baby boy was born they named him Isaac which means 'laughter'.

Sarah said, 'God has given me laughter and made me so happy. God does keep his promises.'

Isaac grew up to be a strong and healthy boy. His parents loved him very much.

One day God spoke to Abraham.

'I want you to take your son Isaac to the mountains. There you must offer his life to me.'

God wanted to be sure that Abraham loved him even more than his own son.

It was a terribly hard thing to ask Abraham to do. But he obeyed.

Early next morning Abraham chopped some firewood and sharpened his knife. Isaac could tell something special was going to happen.

'Can I come with you, Father?' he asked.

'Yes, my child,' Abraham replied. 'You and I shall go and worship God together.'

After a long journey they reached the mountains. Abraham and Isaac began to climb a steep slope.

'Father, how can we worship God when we have nothing to offer him?' asked Isaac.

'God will provide,' answered Abraham.

At the place where God had told Abraham to go, Isaac watched his father build a mound of stones which he covered with the firewood.

Then Abraham turned to his son. There were tears in his eyes. He began to tie Isaac's arms so he could not move.

'What are you doing?' Isaac asked, very frightened.

'Trust me, my child.' Abraham replied.

Isaac held his breath wondering what was going to happen. Abraham picked him up and laid him on top of the wood pile. Then he pulled out his large knife and held it over Isaac's trembling body.

Suddenly a voice from heaven called out:

'Abraham, do not harm the boy. Now I know that you trust me. Look, here is a sheep to put on the fire.'

Abraham spun round and saw a sheep caught in the brambles. He dropped the knife and quickly untied Isaac. Then he took the sheep and offered it to God.

Abraham hugged Isaac as they stood watching the fire. He was so happy.

Then God spoke a second time:

'I promise to make you, and all your children, happy and strong. I will protect you because you have obeyed me. Your family will grow until they become a great nation.'

As they walked down the mountain, Abraham said to Isaac:

'Never forget what has happened today. Remember, you can always trust God.'

Joseph's coat of many colours

WHEN Isaac grew up he became a father and had a son called Jacob. One day God said to Jacob, 'Have lots of children.' And Jacob did. In fact he had twelve children - all boys!

Jacob loved Joseph best but his other sons hated Joseph. They called him names: 'Tell-tale! Dreamer! Show-off!' And they were right.

Jacob had given Joseph a beautiful coat of many colours.

'Look at my coat,' Joseph boasted to his brothers. 'I look much smarter than you!'

'Huh!' they said. 'We don't care.' But really they were jealous.

Another time Joseph told his brothers:

'I dreamt about you last night. You were all bowing down to me.'

'Huh!' they said. 'So you think you're better than us. Show off!'

One day the brothers were looking after Jacob's sheep. They left Joseph behind.

Jacob told Joseph, 'Go and see if your brothers are alright.'

When the brothers saw Joseph coming they said:

'Quick, now's our chance! Let's take his coat and throw him into that empty well.'

Rip! Off came Joseph's new coat. Thud! Joseph landed at the bottom of a deep, dark well.

The brothers sat down to eat. Presently they saw some traders riding towards them on camels.

'Let's sell Joseph to these traders,' the brothers agreed. 'They can buy him for twenty pieces of silver.'

When the traders arrived, the brothers dragged Joseph out of the well and sold him to the men, who were on their way to Egypt.

When it was time to go home, the brothers decided to tell their father a lie.

'Let's pretend Joseph was eaten by a wild animal,' they said.

When Jacob heard the news he couldn't stop crying. He was dreadfully upset.

Meanwhile in Egypt, Joseph was sold to Potiphar, a captain in the King of Egypt's army.

Potiphar liked Joseph. 'I know you're honest,' he said, 'so I'm putting you in charge of my servants.'

But Mrs Potiphar wasn't honest.

'Come and kiss me, Joseph,' she cooed.

'No thanks,' said Joseph and ran off.

Mrs Potiphar was so angry with Joseph she told her husband a lie.

'Joseph kissed me!' she said.

Potiphar was furious and threw Joseph into a deep, dark jail.

The jailors liked Joseph.

'We know you're honest,' they said, 'so we're putting you in charge of the prisoners.'

One night two prisoners had very strange dreams.

'God has told me what your dreams mean,' said Joseph. 'One of you will have his head chopped off. The other will be set free.' And that's exactly what happened.

Two years later, Pharaoh, the King of Egypt, had two very strange dreams. When Joseph heard about them he said:

'God has told me what these dreams mean. There'll be seven years of good harvests then seven years of bad harvests.'

The King of Egypt was delighted and sent for Joseph.

'You're the only person who understands my dreams,' he said, 'so you shall take charge of my land.'

And Joseph became the King's most important helper.

For seven years there were good harvests and Joseph told everyone to store plenty of food. Then came seven bad harvests and Joseph told everyone to share the food.

Joseph was doing really well. But he often thought about his father and wondered whether he would ever see his family again.

Joseph sees his family again

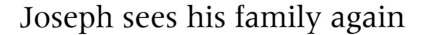

THERE was a great famine in Israel and Jacob and his sons were running out of food.

'Let's go to Egypt,' they said. 'We can get plenty of food there.'

So the brothers went to Egypt to buy food. Except for Benjamin. Jacob loved him the best now and wanted him to stay at home.

When the brothers reached Egypt, they knelt down in front of Joseph, not recognizing him as their long lost brother.

'It's like that dream I had,' thought Joseph. 'But I won't tell them who I am yet. I'll set them a test to see if they've become any nicer.'

'You look like spies to me,' said Joseph. 'Throw them into jail!' he commanded.

Thud! The brothers were thrown into a dark jail.

'It's our own fault,' they groaned. 'We left Joseph to die and now it's our turn.'

After three days, Joseph sent for them.

'You may leave now,' he said, 'except for Simeon. You can have him back when you bring Benjamin to me.'

When Jacob heard the news he was most upset.

'First Joseph, then Simeon. Now you want to take Benjamin. It's all too much,' he sobbed.

'Please let us return,' begged the brothers. 'We promise we'll look after Benjamin.'

At last Jacob agreed. The brothers returned to Egypt and knelt down in front of Joseph.

'It's like my dream again,' thought Joseph, 'but I still won't say who I am. To be quite sure they've changed, I'll set them one more test.'

'You may all leave,' he said. 'Take as much food as you can carry. My servants will fill your sacks.'

Joseph secretly told Abi, his servant, to hide his silver cup in Benjamin's sack. Abi did as he was told.

The brothers had just left when Abi came chasing after them.

'Hey!' he shouted. 'One of you has stolen a silver cup!'

'Open your sacks,' Abi ordered. When Benjamin's sack was opened, Abi found the silver cup. The brothers returned to the palace very worried.

'Please don't punish Benjamin,' they begged Joseph. 'Our father will die if we leave him here.'

Joseph could see they really cared so he took a deep breath and said, 'I am your brother Joseph.'

The brothers could hardly believe it. 'Are you really Joseph?' they gasped.

'It's true,' said Joseph. 'God kept me safe and helped me save many lives. But I forgive you. Now go back to Israel and fetch Jacob.'

When Jacob heard the news he was astonished. But God spoke to him again.

'Don't be frightened, Jacob. Go to Egypt. I'll be with you. One day your people will return to Israel.'

So the whole family moved to Egypt and lived there for many years.

God chooses Moses

Many of the people that God chose to work for him were very ordinary, like you or me.
Moses became a great leader, but he was often scared about doing what God wanted.

BY the time Jacob died, his twelve sons had many children. Joseph and his brothers became fathers and grandfathers. More and more families grew up and lived in Egypt. The Egyptians called them Israelites.

Many years passed. A new King ruled Egypt, King Pharaoh. He was cruel and had never heard of Jacob, Joseph or their God.

'I don't like all these foreigners,' he thought. 'I'll make life really hard for them. They can be my slaves and just do what I tell them.'

So King Pharaoh made his people build new cities and work in the fields. The people moaned but King Pharaoh only made them work harder.

'There are too many of these people,' he complained, 'and they have too many children.'

One day he gave a terrible order. 'Every boy that is born must be killed!'

Now an Israelite woman called Jochebed had a baby boy. She was frightened someone would hear him crying so she decided to hide him in a basket and leave him in the bulrushes by the river. The baby's sister, Miriam, stayed nearby to keep watch.

That day, King Pharaoh's daughter, the Princess, came down to the river.

The baby was crying. 'Waa! Waa!'

'I can hear a baby,' said the Princess. Then she saw the basket.

'Bring me that basket!' she ordered her servant.

When it was opened, they found the baby boy.

'This must be an Israelite baby,' the Princess thought. 'I can't leave him here to die.'

Miriam could see the Princess cared about the baby. Bravely she went up to the Princess.

'Shall I find someone to look after the baby?' she asked.

'Yes, do,' replied the Princess.

Miriam ran to fetch her mother, Jochebed.

'Please look after this baby for me,' said the Princess to Jochebed. 'Call him Moses, which means I took him from the water.'

Jochebed was delighted to have her own son back.

'Thank you, God,' she prayed. 'Now I can bring up Moses myself.'

When Moses grew older he went to live in Pharaoh's palace. He became strong and clever. Still the Israelite people were slaves. God saw how cruel King Pharaoh was to them.

'I'll send someone to rescue my people,' God said. 'Moses is the man to do it. I will appear to Moses myself and speak to him.'

Some time later, Moses was alone in the desert when he saw a bush on fire. He walked up to it. Suddenly he heard a voice.

'Moses, Moses!'

Moses jumped. There was no-one there. Only the burning bush. Moses was terrified. The voice came again!

'Moses, Moses, I want you to take my people away from Egypt.'

Moses gulped. 'Who are you?' he asked.

'I am your God,' replied the voice.

'But what if the people won't come?' Moses said.

'I'll help you,' said God.

'Please send someone else,' pleaded Moses.

'I'll send your older brother Aaron with you,' God said.

'Alright,' said Moses at last. 'I'll go.'

So Moses and Aaron set off together to see the cruel King Pharaoh.

Moses saves the Israelites

BEFORE Moses and Aaron went to meet King Pharaoh, they talked to the Israelite leaders.

'God is going to rescue you!' said Moses.

'Hurrah!' they cheered.

They were very happy.

But King Pharaoh wasn't happy at all.

'I shall never let the Israelites go!' he told Moses and Aaron. 'In fact I'll make them work even harder.'

From then on, King Pharaoh made the Israelites do more and more work. The Israelite leaders were worried.

'We're in big trouble,' they told Moses and Aaron. 'If we don't work hard enough, King Pharaoh will kill us.'

The Israelites were also worried.

'We're going to die.

It's Moses' fault.

God doesn't really care,' they moaned.

Even Moses was worried.

'What's happening?' he asked God. 'King Pharaoh is worse than before. Why did you send me here?'

God replied, 'I will make King Pharaoh free my people. I will save you. I promise.'

But the people didn't believe God.

'God can't help us,' they shouted. 'He doesn't keep his promises!'

'It's time to show Pharaoh my power,' thought God.

So he turned all the water in Egypt red. He sent a plague of frogs. They hopped everywhere. He sent a plague of flies. They buzzed everywhere. He sent a hailstorm. It flattened everything. Then came three whole days of darkness. But still King Pharaoh would not let the Israelites go. So God sent the most terrible plague of all. But first of all he asked the Israelites to do something special.

'Put a sign over your doors so that when my angel passes over, no-one will be harmed.'

The Israelites did as they were told. Then they waited. That night when God's angel passed over he did not harm the Israelites because he saw the sign. But when he passed over the homes without a sign, the firstborn child died. At last King Pharaoh changed his mind.

'Get out of Egypt and never come back!' he yelled.

'Hurrah!' cheered the Israelites.

They rushed about getting ready for their journey. But before they left, God asked the Israelites to do something for him.

'From now on, at the same time each year, you must have a Passover meal,' God said. 'Then you will always remember how I saved you.'

Then God led the Israelites into the desert. He told Moses what would happen next.

'Camp by the Red Sea. Pharaoh will come after you but I will save you.'

Back in his palace, King Pharaoh was furious.

'I wish I'd never let the slaves go! Now I have no-one to do my work. I want them back.'

Very soon King Pharaoh and his army were charging after the Israelites to bring them back again to Egypt.

The Israelites were terrified! In front of them was the Red Sea. Behind them was Pharaoh's army. They were trapped.

'We're going to die.

It's Moses' fault.

God doesn't really care,' they moaned.

'Don't be frightened,' said Moses. 'God will fight for you.'

Suddenly a strong wind began to blow across the sea.

'Look at that!' said the Israelites. 'It's amazing!'

The wind blew right through the middle of the sea and made a dry path!
'Hurry!' said Moses.

The Israelites picked up their things and began to walk through the sea to the other side. No-one even got wet!

King Pharaoh's army was catching up. Nearer and nearer they came. Pharaoh and his men drove into the dry path.

'Now I shall show Pharaoh my power,' said God. And he sent the sea back to its place. The waves poured all over King Pharaoh and his men.

'Help! Help! Help!' The waves came right over their heads until they were all drowned.

'Hurrah! We're safe now!' cried the Israelites. And they began to sing and dance because they were so happy.

Moses teaches God's laws

'WE'RE free!' cried the Israelites. 'Thank God!' After many years the Israelites were no longer slaves in Egypt. God had rescued them and now Moses was leading them to a new land.

First they had to cross a hot, dry, sandy desert. When they got to Mount Sinai they stopped, and God spoke to Moses from the mountain.

'Tell the Israelites they are my special people. I want them to live such good lives that everyone will know how special they are.'

When Moses told the Israelites what God had said, they promised:

'We'll do anything God says.'

Then God said to Moses, 'Tell the people to wash. In three days I will appear to them.'

The people wanted to be as clean as they could be. They scrubbed their hands and faces until they looked fresh and clean. They even scrubbed behind their ears!

Boom! Boom! There was thunder. Crackle! Crackle! There was lightning. Swirl! Swirl! There were clouds of thick smoke. Wobble! Wobble! The ground began to shake.

God had come. The people trembled. Their teeth chattered. Their knees knocked. Then Moses left the Israelites and went back up the mountain where God spoke to him again.

'Listen carefully. I am your God who rescued you from Egypt. This is how my people are to live. These laws are called my Ten Commandments.

Don't worship or pray to any other gods but me.

Don't let anyone or anything be more important than me.

Don't make fun of my name.

Have one day's rest from work each week.

Be polite to your parents.

Don't kill anyone.

When you marry, don't chase after other men or women.

Don't steal.

Don't tell lies.

Don't be greedy for things that don't belong to you.'

God said many more things and Moses listened. Hours passed. Days passed. Moses was away a long time.

The Israelites began to get annoyed. They said to Aaron:

'Moses isn't coming back. Make us another god we can see and touch.'

'Give me your gold ear-rings,' said Aaron.

So the people took off their ear-rings. Aaron melted them down and made a gold statue of a baby cow.

'Here is our god!' the people shouted. 'Let's have a big party for our god!'

Next day they had the biggest, wildest party ever.

But God was watching. He was very angry.

'Please don't be angry,' said Moses. 'Don't forget your promise to give your people a new land.'

God listened to Moses and decided to keep his promise. He gave Moses two stones with his Ten Commandments written on them.

When Moses saw what the people had done he threw the stones down. Smash! They broke into thousands of tiny pieces. Then he took the golden cow and threw it into the fire.

'What happened?' he asked his brother Aaron.

'The people made me throw the gold into the fire and out came a cow,' replied Aaron.

'Do you expect me to believe that!' said Moses. 'You have behaved very badly,' he told everyone. 'I must go and ask God to forgive you.'

When Moses talked to God again, God agreed to write his laws on another two stones. Before Moses left, God made another promise.

'I will do amazing things for my people. Tell them not to make friends with my enemies.'

So Moses went back to the Israelites. His face shone like the sun because he had been close to God.

The Israelites looked at Moses and trembled. Their teeth chattered. Their knees knocked.

'Moses has been with God!' they gasped. 'Let's listen to him.'

So Moses told them the laws God had made and showed them the two stones. For many years Moses taught the people about God and explained that if they followed God's laws he would lead them to a happy life in a new land.

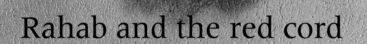

Rahab and the red cord

Whenever God chose to help his people, he wanted them, in return, to trust him and to obey him - these next stories are about Rahab who trusted and Achan who disobeyed.

AFTER Moses died, Joshua became the leader of the Israelites. God told Joshua:

'Be brave and lead my people into the land I promised to give them. Obey my laws and you will succeed.'

But first the Israelites had to take over towns and cities where the people were enemies of God. One of these cities was called Jericho. Not everyone in Jericho was against God. A woman called Rahab believed in him. But Rahab had her own enemies, her neighbours. They often stood at the end of the street gossiping about her.

'Rahab's a strange woman,' they complained. 'She believes in one God.'

'She's always having noisy parties and she invites all kinds of men to her house,' they grumbled.

'We wouldn't trust her,' they agreed.

One day as they stood gossiping, two men walked up to Rahab's door and knocked nervously. The neighbours stared at the men.

'Wonder who they are,' they said. 'They're not from Jericho.'

The neighbours watched closely as Rahab appeared at the door. The strangers were anxious not to be overheard so they spoke softly.

'We've been sent by God's servant, Joshua,' one explained.

'God wants us to take over the city,' added the other.

'I know you're God's people and that your God is powerful,' said Rahab. 'We've heard how God rescued you from slavery in Egypt. Everyone is scared of you. Come in. Make yourselves at home.'

That night the two strangers stayed in Rahab's home. But then the King of

Jericho heard about them and sent his soldiers to arrest the men. Just before the soldiers arrived, Rahab quickly took the men up to the roof and hid them under piles of hay.

'They're not here,' she told the soldiers. 'You've just missed them.'

The soldiers believed her and set off straightaway in search of the men. Climbing to the roof, Rahab gave Joshua's men the good news.

'You're safe now,' she said.

'Thank you, Rahab. Our master will hear how you helped us,' they said.

'Please look after me and my family when you take the city,' Rahab pleaded.

'We promise,' they answered. 'Only do one thing. Hang this red cord from your window. No-one will attack your house if they see this cord.'

Early next morning Rahab helped the men escape by climbing from a window down a rope. The men returned to Joshua and reported back all that had happened.

'Rahab says everyone in Jericho is scared of us,' they said.

'Who is Rahab?' asked Joshua.

'She believes in God and she hid us from the King's soliders,' they answered.

'God has used her to save your lives,' Joshua replied.

That day Rahab's neighbours had plenty to talk about.

'Those two men climbed down a rope this morning. Rahab let them stay all night. It's shocking!' they agreed.

'And now there's a bright red cord hanging out of the window,' they added. 'What *will* everyone say!'

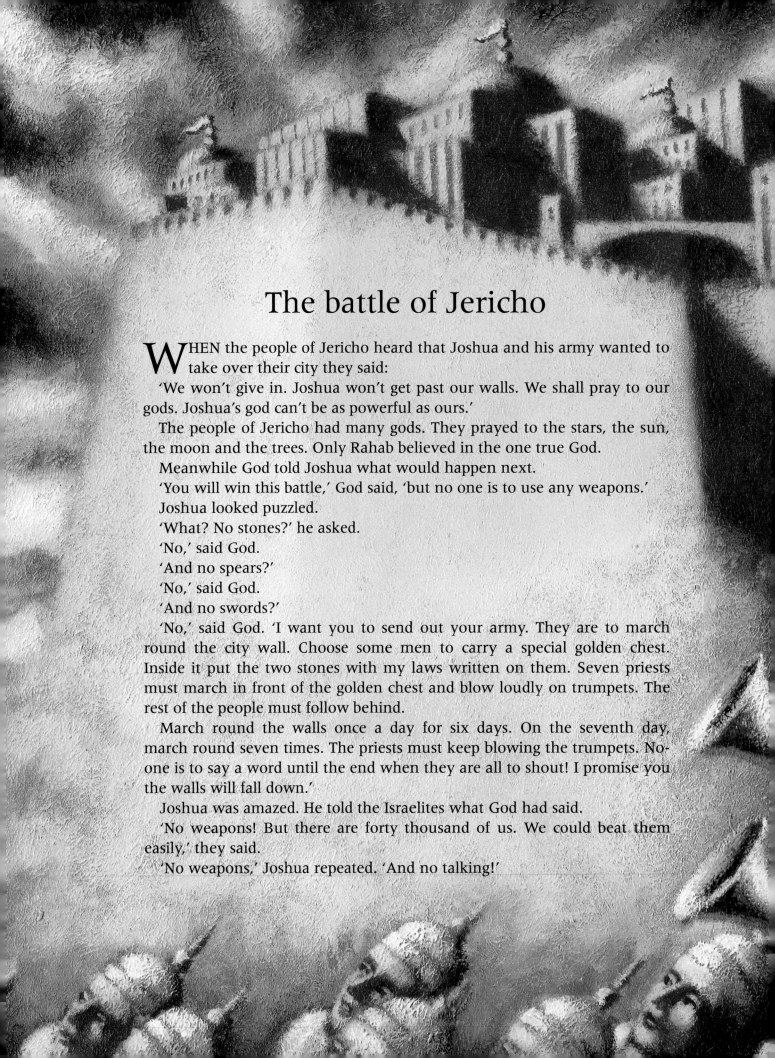

The battle of Jericho

WHEN the people of Jericho heard that Joshua and his army wanted to take over their city they said:

'We won't give in. Joshua won't get past our walls. We shall pray to our gods. Joshua's god can't be as powerful as ours.'

The people of Jericho had many gods. They prayed to the stars, the sun, the moon and the trees. Only Rahab believed in the one true God.

Meanwhile God told Joshua what would happen next.

'You will win this battle,' God said, 'but no one is to use any weapons.'

Joshua looked puzzled.

'What? No stones?' he asked.

'No,' said God.

'And no spears?'

'No,' said God.

'And no swords?'

'No,' said God. 'I want you to send out your army. They are to march round the city wall. Choose some men to carry a special golden chest. Inside it put the two stones with my laws written on them. Seven priests must march in front of the golden chest and blow loudly on trumpets. The rest of the people must follow behind.

March round the walls once a day for six days. On the seventh day, march round seven times. The priests must keep blowing the trumpets. No-one is to say a word until the end when they are all to shout! I promise you the walls will fall down.'

Joshua was amazed. He told the Israelites what God had said.

'No weapons! But there are forty thousand of us. We could beat them easily,' they said.

'No weapons,' Joshua repeated. 'And no talking!'

It really seemed crazy to the Israelites but they agreed to do as God asked.

The army marched at the front. Behind them the priests blew their trumpets. Behind the priests came the golden chest with God's laws inside it. At the back came the rest of the people.

The trumpets made a terrific din but the people didn't make a sound. No-one said a word - which was very hard for some people.

They marched round the walls, once a day for six days. On the seventh day they marched round seven times.

Finally Joshua ordered them to shout. The trumpets sounded again, louder than ever before. The people shouted, louder than they had ever shouted before. The noise was deafening.

Crash! The walls came tumbling down! The people inside couldn't believe their eyes. Joshua's God had beaten them!

'Go and bring out Rahab and her family,' Joshua said. 'Look after them as we promised.'

When Rahab and her family were safe outside the city, Joshua and his men set fire to it. So God wiped out his enemies at Jericho and the news spread throughout the land:

'God is on Joshua's side!'

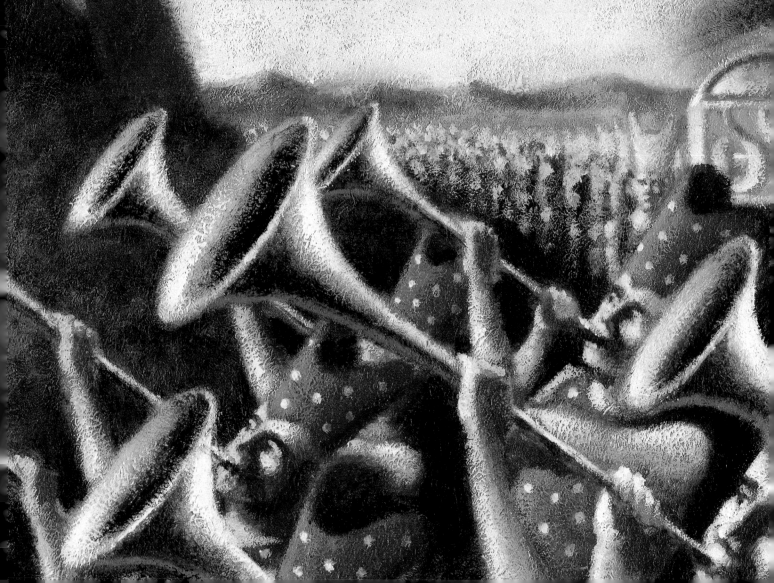

Achan steals from God

AFTER Joshua won the battle at Jericho the Israelites were really pleased. At last they had begun to take over the land God had promised them. It was great to know God was on their side.

'Our next battle is against the city of Ai,' said Joshua. 'But this time we don't need so many men. Ai is only a small place.'

So Joshua took a smaller army to fight the people of Ai. But everything went wrong. The people of Ai fought back and killed thirty-six Israelites.

'Run for your lives!' shouted Joshua.

The Israelites ran back to Jericho. Joshua was very scared and upset.

'We've been beaten,' he told God. 'Where were you?'

God said, 'My people have done something very wrong. They have robbed me. That is why I could not help you. You will not win another battle unless you obey me.'

'Tell me what to do,' Joshua said.

'Tomorrow morning tell the people to come forward, one family at a time. I will pick out the family who has stolen from me.'

Next morning the Israelites gathered together. Joshua spoke to them.

'A terrible wrong has been done. God has been robbed.'

The Israelites gasped. 'Who could do such a thing?' they asked.

Now a man called Achan knew.

'There are so many people. They'll never find out that I did it. I'll pretend I know nothing,' he thought.

One by one, each family came and stood in front of Joshua. Each time Joshua asked God, 'Have they robbed you?'

And each time God replied, 'No.'

But when the family of Zerah came forward, God said:

'This is the family.'

Then one by one each member of Zerah's family came forward. Everyone waited and watched. First came the great grandparents. Then came the grandparents. Then came the parents. Then finally their grown-up son, Achan. When Achan stepped forward, God told Joshua:

'This is the man.'

'Tell me the truth,' said Joshua. 'What have you done?'

'I saw a beautiful cloak, a bar of gold and hundreds of silver coins. I wanted them very much so I stole them and hid them in my tent,' said Achan.

The Israelites gasped.

'Servants, go and see if this is true!' Joshua ordered.

Two men ran off to Achan's tent. They came running back, carrying the cloak, the gold and the silver.

'It's true, master,' they said.

'You have brought trouble to all Israel,' said Joshua. 'You are the only one from forty thousand people who has stolen from God. You must be punished.'

'Achan must be punished!' the people agreed.

So Achan was taken away to be punished.

After this the Israelites won their battles and God helped them to keep the land he had given them.

God calls to Samuel

*The men and women and boys and girls who dared to say they followed God
needed to be very brave. There was no room for cowards in God's army.*

THE Israelites won many battles against their enemies and for a time they
lived in peace in the land God had given them.

Hannah and her husband were Israelites who lived there. Hannah was
very sad. She had been married for a long time but she still had no child.

Hannah prayed to God. 'Please God, I want to be a mother. I want a son.
If you give me a son, I promise you I will let him serve you all his life.'

As she was praying, an old priest called Eli was watching her. 'May God
answer your prayers,' Eli said.

Hannah stopped crying. 'Thank you,' she said, feeling happier.

Some time later Hannah had a baby boy! She called him Samuel. When
Samuel was big enough to feed and dress himself Hannah took him to Eli.

'God answered my prayer,' she said. 'Here is the son I promised him.'

So Samuel lived with Eli, who cared for him. Samuel wanted to please
God very much and loved helping Eli.

Now Eli had two sons of his own. But they were selfish, greedy and cruel.
They were priests like their father but they were bad priests. They lied, they
stole, they chased after women and they were rude to their father.

Eli told his sons:

'I am not pleased with you because you do so many wrong things.'
The two sons laughed.

'How are you going to stop us, you silly old fool?' they said.
Eli didn't know what to say or do. He shook his head and did nothing.

Years passed. Eli grew older and weaker. Samuel grew older and
stronger. Eli's sons grew more selfish and greedy.

One day God told Eli:

'Your sons must be punished. I will choose someone else to be my priest, someone I can trust.'

Eli felt sad but he knew God was right.

One night, after Eli had gone to sleep, Samuel lay awake.

'If Eli needs help I will run to him,' thought Samuel.

'Samuel,' a voice called. Samuel jumped to his feet and ran to Eli.

'Here I am,' said Samuel.

'I didn't call you. Go back to bed,' Eli mumbled. Samuel lay down again.

'Samuel,' the voice called. Samuel sprang up and ran again to Eli.

'Here I am,' he said.

'I didn't call you. Go back to bed,' Eli grumbled. Samuel went back to bed.

'Samuel,' the voice called again.

'There it is again,' thought Samuel. He ran to Eli.

'Here I am,' he said. Now this was the third time Samuel had come to Eli.

'Maybe God is calling you,' said Eli. 'Next time you hear the voice say, "Speak, Lord, and I will listen."'

Samuel nodded. When he was back in bed, God called again:

'Samuel, Samuel.'

This time Samuel replied, 'Speak, Lord, and I will listen.'

'Eli's sons must be punished,' said God. 'They have done many wrong things. Eli did nothing to stop them. They can no longer be priests.'

Next morning Eli called Samuel and asked, 'What did God say?'

Samuel was scared to tell him.

'Tell me the truth Samuel,' said Eli, 'even if it's difficult.'

So Samuel told Eli everything. Eli nodded his head.

'God knows best,' he said.

Not long after, Eli's sons were punished and Samuel became the priest instead. Samuel grew very wise and helped the people to turn back to God. He became one of the greatest leaders the Israelites had ever had.

David fights Goliath

BEFORE Samuel died, God told him to make Saul the first king of the Israelites. Saul was a strong and handsome young man. He fought many battles against the enemies of the Israelites - especially the Philistines.

The Philistines were a fierce, wild bunch of people who didn't believe in the one true God of the Israelites. The fiercest, wildest Philistine was called Goliath. He was nearly three metres tall. No-one dared to fight him, not even Saul.

At this time there was a young shepherd boy called David. He wasn't old enough to fight in the Israelite army. But he was brave. Often wild animals came after his sheep. Bears and lions, prowling and growling.

When David heard the sheep bleating in fright and knew the wild animals were about, he would pick up his catapult and some stones.

Ping! Ping! The stones would whizz through the air.

And the lions and bears would shrink back to their lairs.

Now three of David's brothers were in Saul's army. One day, David's father told him to take some food to his brothers.

David arrived just in time to see the Israelites and the Philistines lining up for battle. There was one Philistine who stood out because he was taller than everyone else. It was Goliath.

David stared at him in amazement.

Goliath walked forward, his heavy armour glistening in the sun. Clank! Clank! Clank! He looked like a big metal monster.

'Who dares to come and fight me?' Goliath boomed.

The Israelites took one look, turned and fled.

'Who does he think he is?' said David. 'I'm not scared of him.'

The Israelite soldiers laughed:

'Listen to the boy. Goliath's twice as big as you. He'll eat you for breakfast.'

When Saul heard what David had said, he asked to meet him.

'I'll go and fight Goliath,' said David. 'God will help me.'

'You're far too small,' said Saul. 'He's twice your size.'

'I'm not frightened of bears or lions. And I'm not frightened of this Goliath.'

'Alright, young man,' said Saul. 'You may go. Here, take my armour.'

Saul gave David a heavy helmet and a big coat of armour. Clank! Clank! Clank! David could hardly move.

'I can't fight in these,' David mumbled from inside the helmet. So he took the armour off.

Then he picked up his catapult and five, smooth, round stones. Goliath watched in amazement as David walked towards him.

'Ho! Ho! Ho!' he laughed loudly. 'So your God needs boys to fight his battles does he?'

'My God will help me beat you,' said David.

'Ho! Ho! Ho!' Goliath boomed. 'You must think I'm stupid!'

Now Goliath was very big but he couldn't move very fast. David ran up quickly and pulled his catapult back as far as it would go.

Ping! The stone whizzed through the air. Thwack! It hit Goliath so hard it made a big dent in his head.

Goliath fell flat on his face, dead!

'Hurrah!' the Israelites cheered.

As soon as the Philistines saw Goliath was dead they turned and ran. The Israelites charged after them. From that day on, David stayed with Saul and helped him to win many more battles. When Saul died, David became king and ruled over the Israelites.

King Solomon

WHEN King David died, his son Solomon became king of the Israelites. Now God made Solomon very wise. One day two women came to Solomon. One of them said:

'Your Majesty, this woman and I live in the same house. We both had our own babies. Her baby was born two days after mine. One night this woman put her baby in her bed and fell asleep. By mistake she rolled over on top of her baby and the baby died. Then she put her dead baby in my bed and took away my baby.'

'That's not true!' cried the other woman. 'The dead baby is hers!'

'Oh no he isn't!' said the first woman.

'Oh yes he is!' the other replied.

'Stop!' shouted Solomon. 'Bring me a sword. Will you stop arguing if I cut the baby in two and give each of you a half.'

'Please don't kill the baby,' the real mother cried out. 'Give him to her.'

But the other woman said, 'No! Go ahead. Cut him in half.'

Then Solomon said, 'No-one shall kill the baby. Give him to the first woman. She is the real mother.'

When everyone heard this story they agreed, 'God has made Solomon very wise.'

Not long after, King Solomon built a magnificent temple in the city of Jerusalem where Israelites could go to worship God. It was built using the best materials and inside it was filled with beautiful things made from gold, silver and bronze. The two stone slabs which God had given Moses were placed inside.

God was pleased with the temple. He told Solomon:

'If you obey me I will live in this temple and will never leave my people.'

Time passed. King Solomon died. The Israelites began to forget about God. They made false gods from stone and gold. They broke God's laws and

prayed to the stars. God sent messengers to tell the Israelites to obey him but they would not listen.

'I will have to punish them,' God thought sadly. So God let a powerful people called the Babylonians attack Jerusalem.

The King of Babylon, who was called Nebuchadnezzar, and his army marched into Jerusalem. His army smashed the city walls, burnt down the temple and took everything made of gold, silver or bronze!

Nebuchadnezzar's soldiers also killed many Israelites and took thousands of others to Babylon, miles away from the land God had given them. The Israelites were terribly shocked.

'We've lost the land God promised us and we've been beaten by people who do not follow him,' they said. 'We thought God would never let anyone attack Jerusalem.'

In Babylon Nebuchadnezzar was kind to the Israelites and let them follow their God. The Israelites said:

'We've lost our land and temple. All we have left are God's laws. Let's turn back to God and obey him.'

But others said, 'Now we have no temple maybe God has left us.'

Now God knew what the people were thinking. So he sent Ezekiel, a man he could trust, with this message.

'Say I am still with them,' said God. 'One day they will return to the land I gave them. I will help them to obey me. They will be my people and I will be their God. I will never leave them.'

When the people heard this they were very happy. They laughed and sang for joy. More importantly they said sorry to God and prayed:

'Thank you God for not leaving us. Please help us to love you and obey all your laws always. Amen.'

Daniel in the lions' den

WHEN King Nebuchadnezzar's army attacked Jerusalem, some Israelites were taken away to Babylon. The King picked out some young Israelite men.

'You will be my servants,' he ordered. 'You will study books about Babylon and become very wise.'

Four of these men were called Daniel, Shadrach, Meshach and Abednego. Time passed. Daniel and his three friends studied and became cleverer than all the wise men in Babylon.

One night the King had such a bad dream he could not sleep. He was so worried about it that he sent for his chief wise men.

'Tell me what I dreamt last night and what it means!' he ordered.

The wise men gasped. 'Your Majesty, please tell us the dream first or we can't help you.'

'If *you* don't tell *me* the dream I'll have you killed!' he shouted.

'But only the gods could tell you that and they're not here,' they replied, horrified.

Nebuchadnezzar was furious.

'Tomorrow all wise men will be put to death!'

When Daniel heard his life was in danger, he went to the King.

'Your Majesty, please give me time to find out your dream,' he begged. Nebuchadnezzar agreed.

Daniel went straight to his three friends.

'We must pray and ask God to show us the King's dream,' he explained.

That night God told Daniel the meaning of the dream.

Next morning Daniel spoke to Nebuchadnezzar:

'God has shown me your dream.'

As the King listened, he began to smile. Everything Daniel said was true.

'Your God must be the one true living God, for all you have said is right,' Nebuchadnezzar said. 'Now you will be my special helper.'

Years passed and a new King, Darius, ruled in Babylon. Daniel was still the most important helper. But the other helpers in the palace were jealous.

'Let's get Daniel into trouble,' they said. 'He's such a goody goody.'

So they plotted and went to King Darius.

'Your Majesty, may all your people pray only to you. May anyone who prays to any other god be thrown to the lions!'

Darius liked this idea. So a law was passed. 'No-one is to pray to anyone except King Darius. By Order!'

When Daniel heard this, he went straight home and prayed to God. People outside could see him because he left his windows wide open.

Daniel's enemies watched, then went off to tell the King. Darius hated the idea of sending Daniel to the lions. But Daniel had broken the law. The helpers threw Daniel into the lions' den.

'Grrrrrrr!' the lions growled.

'May your God help you,' said King Darius.

'Grrrrrrr! Grrrrrrr!' the lions growled louder and louder.

King Darius went back to the palace. 'Poor Daniel,' he thought. 'The lions will tear him to pieces.'

Next day Darius went back to the lions' den. And there was Daniel, alive and well!

'Your Majesty, God sent an angel to stop the lions eating me up!' he cried.

Darius was overjoyed. Daniel was set free straightaway and went back to live in the palace. The jealous helpers were thrown to the lions because the king was so angry with them.

Elijah prays for rain

This story shows that things that are impossible for us are possible for God.

OVER the years, the Israelites had many different kings and leaders. One of these was called King Ahab. He was one of the worst leaders Israel had ever had. He didn't obey or love God. In fact he loved his wife Jezebel more than he loved God. Queen Jezebel was a bad-tempered woman.

'Your God is a load of rubbish!' she shouted.

'Yes dear,' said Ahab.

Jezebel believed in Baal, the god of war and weather. She wanted all the Israelites to believe in him too.

'Bow down and worship my god Baal!' she ordered.

'Yes dear,' said Ahab.

'Kill all the men who teach people to love and obey your God!' she yelled.

'Yes dear,' said Ahab.

Soon all the Israelites were bowing down to Baal. God was very angry and sent the one man he could trust, Elijah, to give Ahab this warning:

'The one, true, living God says there will be no rain unless I say so.'

Three years passed. And there was no rain. It was scorchingly hot. The grass, the trees and the crops all died. Ahab was furious.

'When I see that Elijah again, I'll kill him!' he said.

One day God sent Elijah to talk to Ahab.

'The time has come for a competition between my God and your god. Call all the Israelites together. Meet me at Carmel mountain,' said Elijah.

Ahab agreed. He called together the Israelites and over four hundred men who taught people to follow Baal. Elijah stood alone.

'Whose side are you on? God's or Baal's?' Elijah asked. No-one spoke.

Elijah went on. 'Build a bonfire. We'll each call on our god to set it alight.'

First King Ahab's men called on Baal. They leapt about and danced. They made lots of noise and got very excited. Elijah watched.

Hours passed. Nothing happened.

'Shout louder,' said Elijah. 'Maybe your god is asleep or on holiday.'

Ahab's men made more noise and danced even harder. Soon they were worn out. Still nothing happened.

Then Elijah said, 'Build a mound of stone. Dig a ditch around the bottom. Put the firewood on top. Then pour twelve barrels of sea-water on the wood.'

'But the wood will go all soft and soggy,' they argued.

'Just do as I ask,' said Elijah.

So they poured on the sea-water. The wood became all soft and soggy. The water filled the ditch.

Then Elijah prayed. 'Please God. Show these people you are a living God.'

Crackle! Crackle! Sizzle! Sizzle! The bonfire burst into flame. The fire was so hot the stones began to melt. The water dried up in the ditch.

The people fell on their knees.

'God is alive!' they cried.

Then Elijah said, 'Take the teachers of Baal away to be punished.'

He looked at Ahab. 'Go back to your palace. It's going to rain.'

Ahab jumped back in his chariot and headed for home.

Elijah knelt down to pray for rain.

Soon a tiny rain cloud appeared in the sky. It grew bigger and bigger until the whole sky turned black.

Pitter, patter. The rain fell gently.

Splitter, splatter. The rain fell more heavily.

Bing! Boing! The rain fell so hard it bounced off the ground.

It was the biggest downpour they had seen in years!

For a time the people believed and obeyed God. But this did not last. Many of them forgot all about him. Elijah kept on telling them about the one, true, living God but many people went back to their old gods.

Esther saves her people

LONG after the days of Elijah the Israelites were unsettled, many of them living in different places. Some of them lived in Babylon for many years. Eventually a King called Cyrus said to these Israelites:

'You can go back to Jerusalem if you wish.'

'Hurrah!' they cried.

But they didn't all return to Jerusalem. Some went to Persia. By this time the Israelites were known as Jews. Many years later, another King, called Xerxes, reigned over them.

Xerxes was very rich and lived in a splendid palace. The time came when he was looking for a wife. He invited hundreds of women from all over Persia to see who he liked best.

Esther was a beautiful Jewish girl. Her parents were dead so her cousin Mordecai brought her up. When Xerxes saw Esther he fell in love.

'Wow!' he thought. 'She is the one for me.'

After the wedding, Xerxes gave a big party. Mordecai hoped Esther was happy. He went to the palace each day to listen to any news. One day as he sat by the palace gates he heard two soldiers talking.

'Let's kill King Xerxes,' one said to the other.

'I must tell Esther to warn the King,' thought Mordecai.

As soon as Esther heard, she told Xerxes what Mordecai had said. Xerxes had the soldiers punished but he forgot to thank Mordecai.

Now the King's most important helper was Haman. He hated the Jews.

'Why can't they be like us,' he snarled. 'We don't pray to God or follow his silly rules.'

One day Haman said to Xerxes:

'There is a bunch of people who have their own laws and do not obey you. They must be killed.'

'Whatever you say, Haman,' Xerxes agreed.

So Haman made a new law. 'All Jews, men, women and children to be killed. By Order!'

On hearing this, Mordecai cried out loud. When Esther heard that Mordecai was sad she sent a servant to find what was wrong.

'Mordecai says Haman has ordered all Jews to be killed,' the servant explained. 'Mordecai wants you to ask the King to stop this terrible thing.'

'But it is strictly forbidden to go to the King without being asked,' thought Esther. 'He could have me put to death.' She felt very worried.

Then Mordecai sent Esther a message:

'Remember you are Jewish too. If you do nothing you may be killed. Maybe God will use you to save the Jews?'

Esther knew Mordecai was right. Dressed in her royal robes, she bravely went to the palace where the King was sitting on his throne.

'What is Esther doing?' thought the King. 'I haven't asked to see her. Doesn't she know I could have her killed for this?'

'If it please Your Majesty, I would like you and Haman to come to a special dinner,' Esther said.

Xerxes smiled. 'We shall be delighted to come,' he said.

Haman felt on top of the world.

'Everything is going well for me,' he thought. But then he met Mordecai.

'I don't like that man. I'll get my men to hang him,' he decided.

That night Xerxes couldn't get to sleep so he asked his servant to read the palace records. The servant came to the story about Mordecai and the plot to murder Xerxes.

'Has this man been thanked?' asked Xerxes.

'No, your Majesty,' replied the servant.

Just then Haman appeared.

'How should I reward someone who has helped me?' asked Xerxes.

Now Haman thought Xerxes was talking about himself.

'I'd give him a crown to wear, a royal gown, the best horse and let him ride through the city,' said Haman.

'A good idea. Go and do that for Mordecai the Jew,' Xerxes ordered.

Haman was shocked. How he hated doing all these things for Mordecai!

That evening Xerxes and Haman sat down to eat with Esther.

'What present can I give you?' Xerxes asked Esther.

'Please save the lives of my people, the Jews,' said Esther.

'Who wants to kill them?' Xerxes replied.

'This horrid man Haman!' Esther declared.

Xerxes was furious.

'You will hang for this!' he shouted at Haman.

So it was Haman who died instead of Mordecai. As for Mordecai he now became the King's special helper.

The Jews were so happy that they held a big party to celebrate and they have never forgotten Esther's courage in risking her life for them.

Isaiah learns of a new king

The Jewish people knew they could look forward to the coming of a new king who would save them, but they didn't know when he would come.

ISAIAH was a Jewish man who lived in Jerusalem. He was a prophet and through him God spoke to the people.

God told Isaiah what would happen to the Jews in the future and about the birth of a new King who would be the best King ever. God asked Isaiah to give this message to the Jews. It was a strange message but sometimes God speaks in a way that people don't always understand.

'There will be a time of big trouble. People will hate me. But the trouble will come to an end.'

'I don't like the sound of that,' thought Isaiah.

'Then wonderful things will happen in the land called Galilee. The people who live in the dark will see a great light. The people of Israel will be so happy. They will be as happy as farmers who have had the best harvest in their lives.'

'That sounds much better,' thought Isaiah.

'I will stop the things that make my people sad,' said God. 'I will win the battle against the people who keep the Jews as their slaves.

There will be no more fighting.

There will be no more killing.

A special son will be born!

He will be your ruler.

He will be called Wonderful.

He will be like a best friend who gives good advice.

He will be called Mighty God, The Father who lives for ever and ever, The Prince of Peace.'

'This is great news for the people,' thought Isaiah.

God went on with his message.

'His power will grow stronger and stronger. He will rule fairly and wisely. He will be a perfect King. I, the God of heaven, will make sure all this comes true.'

'This just gets better and better,' thought Isaiah. 'I can't wait until the new King comes. I wonder what he'll be like?'

Jesus is born

The last thing that the Jewish people expected
was for their new king to be born in a dirty stable. It's hardly surprising
that only a few people recognised him!

MARY was very excited. She was getting married! Mary was a young Jewish girl who lived in the town of Nazareth. Soon she would be the wife of Joseph, the local carpenter.

But one day an astonishing thing happened. Mary saw a terrific flash of light and then she heard an angel.

'God is with you. He has chosen you. You are very special.'

'What does this mean?' thought Mary.

'Don't be frightened. You are going to have a baby boy. You will call him Jesus.'

'I don't understand,' said Mary. 'I'm not married to Joseph yet.'

'You will have a baby by the power of God,' said the angel. 'He will be God's promised king. He will reign for ever and ever. Your cousin Elizabeth is going to have a baby too. Anything is possible with God.'

'I am willing to do whatever God wants,' said Mary. 'May everything you said come true.' Then the angel disappeared.

When Joseph heard Mary was going to have a baby he was very worried.

'People will think I am the father,' he thought. 'And that's not true.'

One night Joseph had an amazing dream. An angel spoke to him.

'Joseph, don't be afraid to marry Mary. The baby is God's son. He will be called Jesus and show people that God forgives them.'

After that Joseph didn't worry any more. He loved Mary and he loved God. He would do as God said.

Meanwhile Mary decided to visit her cousin, Elizabeth. After a long walk she arrived at Elizabeth's house. Elizabeth was surprised to see her.

'Mary!' she cried. 'As soon as you spoke, my baby jumped for joy inside me. God has chosen you to be the mother of his son!'

'How does Elizabeth know that?' Mary wondered. 'God must have told her my news.'

So Mary asked Elizabeth lots of questions and they talked about all the amazing things that God was doing. Mary stayed with Elizabeth for three months then went back to Joseph. Soon after, Elizabeth had a baby boy called John.

Mary and Joseph were really pleased to hear about baby John. God had kept his promise and soon it would be their turn. But first they had to travel to Bethlehem to sign a register so the Roman ruler, who was called Emperor Augustus, knew who lived in his land.

It was a long, hard journey for Mary because it was nearly time to have her baby. She rode on a donkey while Joseph walked slowly beside her. It was very dark and late when they arrived in Bethlehem.

'Sorry we're so late,' said Joseph to the inn keeper, 'but we need a place to stay.'

'I'm afraid we're all booked up. You'll have to sleep in the stable,' he replied.

It was very dark and smelly in the stable. There wasn't much room either. There were sheep and cattle and donkeys in there sleeping on the straw. Joseph tied the donkey up while Mary found a space and lay down on the crackly straw. And that's where baby Jesus was born.

Mary wrapped him in strips of cloth and laid him in a manger. Only Joseph was there to see Jesus born. But God was watching too.

The shepherds go to Bethlehem

'I'M fed up being a shepherd,' said young David.
'It's boring,' agreed Nathan.
'I've been a shepherd fifty years and it's never been exciting,' sighed old Joe.

David and Nathan pulled a face.

'It's going to be a cold night again,' said David.

'Another cold, boring night,' said Nathan.

Suddenly there was a terrific noise of a mighty wind and a brilliant flash of light! All around them was a dazzling bright light and in the middle stood a beautiful, shining angel.

'Don't be frightened,' said the angel. 'I have the most exciting news in the whole world. Today, in the town of Bethlehem, a special baby has been born. He will offer forgiveness to everyone. You will find him wrapped in strips of cloth, lying in a manger.'

The shepherds clung to one another, shaking with fear. Then hundreds of other shining angels appeared. The sky was full of them.

'Glory to God! Peace to all who love him!' they sang.

Then suddenly they disappeared. It was dark and quiet again.

'Goodness!' said David.

'I've been a shepherd fifty years and nothing like that has happened before,' said old Joe.

'That was fantastic!' said Nathan. 'God's angels spoke to us! We must go and find this baby!'

Everyone agreed. They jumped up and began to race down the hill towards Bethlehem.

Mary and Joseph were so surprised to see the shepherds.

'Who told you we were here?' Joseph asked.

'God's angels told us!' they said.

Mary and Joseph looked at each other. They knew all about angels. The shepherds were so excited. They couldn't wait to tell their friends what had happened.

'And we thought being a shepherd was boring,' said David and Nathan.

'This has been the most exciting day in my life,' said old Joe, beaming.

The three wise men visit Jesus

KING Herod was a very worried man. Three wise men who studied the stars were telling people a new king had been born. But Herod didn't want another king in his land.

'I'm the king,' he thought. 'I don't want anyone else being king. I'll put a stop to this.'

In secret, he sent for the wise men whose names were Caspar, Melchior and Balthasar.

'When you find the new king, please tell me where he is, then I can take him a gift,' he lied.

'Certainly, Your Majesty,' they said.

That night the wise men looked out for the star they had been following.

'There it is!' shouted Melchior.

'And it's not moving tonight. We must be very close,' said Caspar.

The star hovered and sparkled above the place where Jesus had been born.

When the wise men saw Jesus they knelt down in the straw.

'We've brought gifts for the new king,' they said. 'Gold, perfume and spices.'

'Thank you,' said Mary and Joseph, smiling. 'But who are you?'

'We are wise men who come from the east, many miles from here,' Balthasar explained.

'How did you know we were here?' Joseph asked.

'We followed a shining star,' they replied.

The wise men found it hard to fall asleep that night because they were so excited that they had found Jesus.

'Won't Herod be pleased when he hears our news?' they said to one another.

But that night an angel spoke to them in a dream.

'Don't tell Herod about baby Jesus. Go back home at once.' So next morning the wise men left Bethlehem.

When Herod heard the wise men had gone, he was furious.

'When I find this child I'll kill him!' he shouted.

But that night an angel spoke to Joseph in a dream.

'Don't stay here any longer. Jesus is in danger. Go quickly to Egypt. You'll be safe there,' he said.

Joseph woke Mary and told her the news.

'We must leave straightaway,' he said.

'But it's past midnight,' Mary replied.

'There's no time to lose,' said Joseph.

So, in the middle of the night, they crept out of the stable and began the long walk to Egypt. They didn't know if they would ever return home.

The family lived in Egypt for several years until King Herod died. Then one night an angel spoke to Joseph in a dream.

'It's safe to go back home now,' he said.

So Mary and Joseph and young Jesus returned to their home in Nazareth.

Jesus is found in the temple

IT was holiday time and young Jesus and his family were going away. Every year in the spring they went to Jerusalem for the Passover festival. At Passover every Jewish family killed a lamb and ate a special meal. This reminded them of how God rescued his people when they were slaves in Egypt.

Jesus loved going to Jerusalem. It was so much busier and more exciting than Nazareth. There was a market place, a stadium, a palace and a huge Jewish temple.

'There'll be lots of people about,' Mary said to Jesus. 'Don't wander off or you'll get lost.' Jesus nodded.

'Now you're twelve you can walk with the bigger boys,' said Joseph.

Many of Jesus' friends and neighbours were going to Jerusalem too. The women and little children walked at the front, while the men and older boys followed behind. Jesus and his friends chased each other and ran around at the back.

When they arrived, Jerusalem was crowded with people. Soon the Passover began. There was plenty of food and drink and dancing and singing. Everyone had a great time.

When it was time to go home, the women set off first again and the men and boys followed. Except for Jesus. He stayed behind to talk to the teachers at the temple.

Everyone was chattering and laughing together. No-one noticed Jesus was missing. That night the crowd stopped to set up camp.

'Have you seen Jesus?' Joseph asked Mary.

'I thought he was with you,' she replied.

'And I thought he was with you,' said Joseph.

So Mary and Joseph hurried all the way back to Jerusalem.

'Where on earth can he be?' they wondered.

When they arrived, they searched the whole city. Jesus was nowhere to be seen.

'Let's try the temple,' suggested Mary.

The temple's huge cream stone walls with their marble and gold decorations sparkled in the sunshine. It was full of people. And there in the middle of the crowds sat Jesus, talking to the Jewish teachers.

'Jesus!' Mary called. 'How could you do this? Your father and I have been so worried. We've been looking for you everywhere!'

'But I wasn't lost,' Jesus replied. 'Didn't you know I would be in my heavenly Father's house?'

Mary and Joseph didn't know what to say. A teacher turned to them.

'Your child is wiser than any child I have ever known,' he said. 'He must be very special.'

Mary and Joseph looked at each other. Yes, Jesus *was* very special.

'Come, Jesus. It's time to go home,' said Joseph.

So Jesus returned with Mary and Joseph to Nazareth. Although his parents didn't really understand it, they never forgot what Jesus said.

Jesus is baptised and tested

*Before Jesus could begin his special work
he had to be sure that he was strong enough to meet all the tough times that lay ahead.
He also needed a group of followers who would help him.*

JESUS grew up to be a fine strong man. He became a carpenter like his father Joseph. But God had always planned a special life for him.

When he was about thirty years old, Jesus left his workshop in Nazareth and went down to the river Jordan to meet John, the son of Elizabeth.

John was teaching people a special message.

'God's king is coming soon. Get ready,' he told them. 'Be baptised and show you are sorry for disobeying God.'

Many people were really sorry and wanted to make a clean start. John was baptising them in the river.

When John saw Jesus, he knew at once that God's king had come.

Jesus walked into the water and stood in front of John, waiting to be baptised.

'*I* need to be baptised by *you*,' said John. 'Not you by me.'

But Jesus answered, 'This is what God wants.'

So John baptised Jesus. As Jesus came up out of the water a white dove came down from the heavens and settled on his head.

Then God spoke from heaven.

'This is my only son whom I have chosen to do my special work.'

After this God sent Jesus into the desert alone to be tested by the devil. It was empty, dry and hot. Jesus had nothing to eat for forty days.

Then the devil, God's enemy, came to test Jesus.

'He must be feeling very hungry,' the devil thought. 'Let's see if he'll use his powers to feed himself.'

'If you are God's son,' he said, 'turn these stones into bread.'

Although Jesus was starvingly hungry, he replied:

'There's more to life than food. To obey God is more important.'

'Bah!' grumbled the devil. 'I'll have to try something else.'

He took Jesus to a very high place and said:

'Let's see if God really will protect you. Throw yourself down!'
But Jesus replied, 'God says do not give me stupid tests.'
'Bah!' grumbled the devil. 'I'll have to try again.'
'Kneel at my feet and I will give you all the riches in the world.'
Now Jesus knew the devil could do this but he said:
'I will only kneel at the feet of God and obey him.'
By this time the devil was furious.
'I'm not getting anywhere with this Jesus,' he grumbled.
'But I won't be beaten. I'll make him disobey
God somehow, some day. I'll be back.'
And off he went.

Jesus calls his first disciples

When Jesus left the desert he went back home to Nazareth and began teaching people about God.

One day he decided to go to Lake Galilee and talk to the people there.

'He's a wonderful teacher,' the people said. 'We could go on listening to him all day.'

More and more people came to hear Jesus. The crowds grew so big he could hardly move.

In order to have more room, Jesus climbed into an empty fishing boat. It belonged to a fisherman called Peter.

'Will you push me out into the lake?' Jesus asked Peter.

'Of course,' said Peter, and he pushed the boat out into the water.

Jesus sat down and Peter watched as Jesus began to talk. The crowd listened to every word.

'I wish I could teach like that,' thought Peter.

When Jesus had finished he called to Peter:

'If you push the boat out further you'll catch lots of fish.'

Peter frowned. 'What does Jesus know about fishing?' he thought. 'He's probably never caught a fish in his life!'

'I promise that you'll catch lots of fish,' Jesus repeated.

'The men worked hard all night and they didn't even catch a tiddler,' Peter answered. 'I don't think it'll work but we'll give it one more try.'

Peter, his brother Andrew and the other men pushed the boat out further and threw their nets into the water. Splosh!

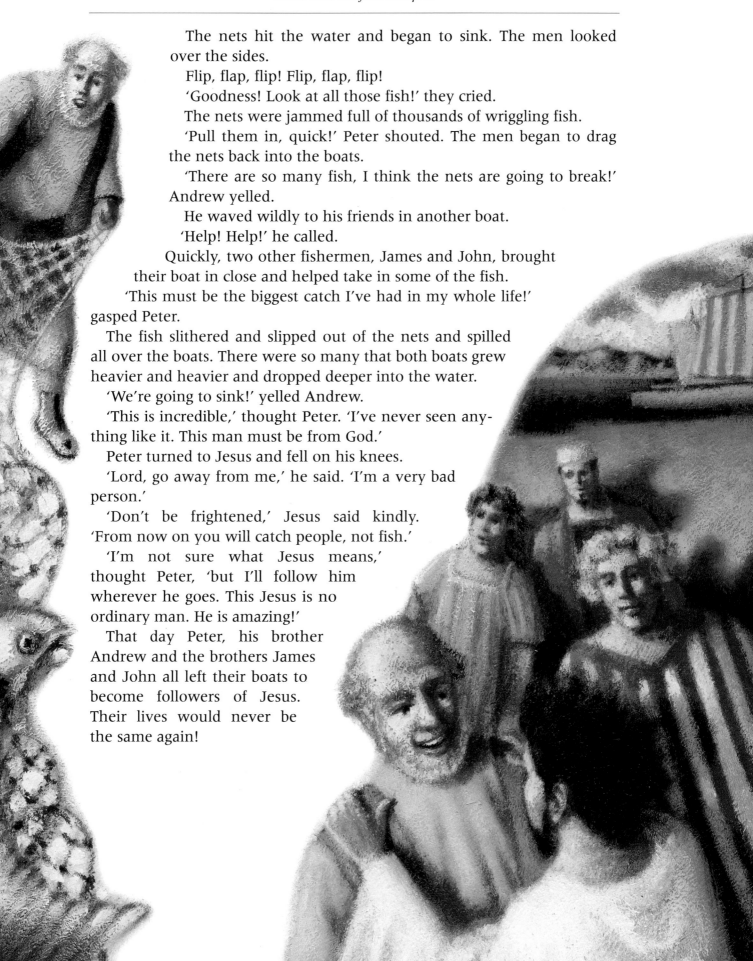

The nets hit the water and began to sink. The men looked over the sides.

Flip, flap, flip! Flip, flap, flip!

'Goodness! Look at all those fish!' they cried.

The nets were jammed full of thousands of wriggling fish.

'Pull them in, quick!' Peter shouted. The men began to drag the nets back into the boats.

'There are so many fish, I think the nets are going to break!' Andrew yelled.

He waved wildly to his friends in another boat.

'Help! Help!' he called.

Quickly, two other fishermen, James and John, brought their boat in close and helped take in some of the fish.

'This must be the biggest catch I've had in my whole life!' gasped Peter.

The fish slithered and slipped out of the nets and spilled all over the boats. There were so many that both boats grew heavier and heavier and dropped deeper into the water.

'We're going to sink!' yelled Andrew.

'This is incredible,' thought Peter. 'I've never seen anything like it. This man must be from God.'

Peter turned to Jesus and fell on his knees.

'Lord, go away from me,' he said. 'I'm a very bad person.'

'Don't be frightened,' Jesus said kindly. 'From now on you will catch people, not fish.'

'I'm not sure what Jesus means,' thought Peter, 'but I'll follow him wherever he goes. This Jesus is no ordinary man. He is amazing!'

That day Peter, his brother Andrew and the brothers James and John all left their boats to become followers of Jesus. Their lives would never be the same again!

Jesus calms the storm

Jesus did many amazing things which we call miracles.
We can never explain them but they show just how powerful
and marvellous God is.

JESUS had spent nearly all day teaching a crowd of people by the side of Lake Galilee. Now it was beginning to grow dark.

'It will soon be nightfall,' Jesus said to his special friends. 'Come, let's go across to the other side of the lake.'

Jesus walked over the crunchy gravel towards the boats which were bobbing up and down in the water. He climbed into one of the boats, sat down at the far end and waited for his friends to join him.

Peter stood waist deep in the water, trying to steady the boat. It rocked from side to side as the men scrambled in.

'Mind your big feet,' grumbled Peter as the boat lurched about. Once they were all in, Peter pushed the boat out into the lake and climbed aboard.

It had been a long, tiring day for Jesus. He lay back with his head on a cushion, closed his eyes and soon he was fast asleep.

As Peter watched the sail, he noticed it was filling out more and more.

'There's a storm brewing,' he thought.

He was right. Within minutes a fierce wind was whipping up the waves so that water was spilling into the boat.

The men tried scooping out the water as fast as they could. Faster and faster they worked but the water kept coming. The wind blew harder and harder. Enormous white waves crashed over their heads.

'We're going to drown! We're going to drown!' the men cried. Peter, who was soaked to the skin, staggered over to Jesus who was still sleeping.

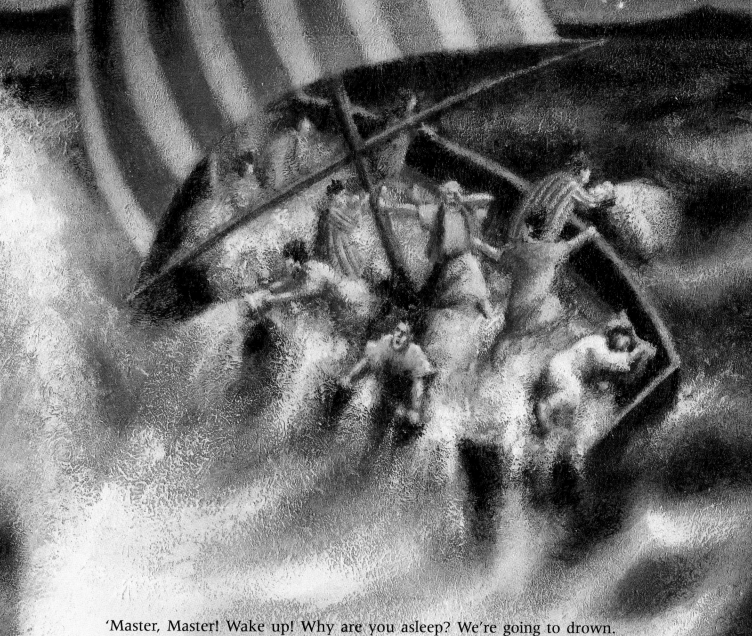

'Master, Master! Wake up! Why are you asleep? We're going to drown. Don't you care?' Peter shook Jesus by the shoulders.

Jesus opened his eyes. Another large spray of water swept over the sides. The roaring seas tossed the boat wildly.

Jesus sprang to his feet and shouted loudly:

'Winds and waves, be quiet! I command you, be still!'

At once the wind dropped. The sea became calm and smooth. There was peace. The men were astonished and stood open-mouthed, staring at Jesus.

'Why were you frightened?' he asked them. 'Don't you know that I care about you?'

No-one replied, because Jesus had told them many times that there was no need to be afraid because he loved them. His friends looked down, feeling a little foolish and ashamed.

Jesus smiled. 'It's alright. Just remember, you'll always be safe with me.'

Jesus heals the paralysed man

NEWS about Jesus spread fast. Everyone wanted to hear the new teacher. People came from far and near to listen to him.

Even the Pharisees came. They were Jewish teachers, like Jesus, but they were very very strict. They made so many rules, it was hard work being a Jew.

One day, Jesus visited a small house in the town of Capernaum. So many people were squashed inside there was no room to move.

'Let us through! We must see Jesus!' a voice cried.

Outside, four men stood at the door, carrying a man on a stretcher. No-one moved.

'It's no use, no-one will budge,' said Ben from his stretcher.

'Wait! I've had an idea,' cried one of Ben's friends. 'Let's go round the side.'

The four men shuffled round the corner of the house. In front of them was an outside staircase which led up on to the roof.

Carefully they climbed up, one step at a time. When they reached the roof, Ben asked:

'What are you going to do?'

'Dig!' said his friend, who dropped on to his knees and began to dig out the roof tiles. The other men copied and soon they had made a hole in the roof.

Down below, they could see Jesus talking to the crowd.

'Keep digging, friends,' called Ben.

Little by little the hole grew bigger.

'What's happening down there?' asked Ben, who by now was feeling a little worried.

'You'll soon find out,' said his friends.

Before Ben could say a word, his friends had picked him up and were slowly lowering him down through the roof until he landed safely at the feet of Jesus. Jesus smiled. He knew these men must really believe that he could help them.

'My friend,' Jesus said to Ben, 'you are forgiven for all the things you have done wrong.'

The crowd gasped.

'Who does Jesus think he is?' thought the Pharisees. 'How dare he forgive someone. Only God can do that.'

But Jesus knew what they were thinking.

'Which is easier to do?' he asked. 'To say "You are forgiven", or "Get up and walk?"'

No-one dared answer.

Jesus said, 'So that you know I can do both, I say, "Get up and walk!"'

The crowd gasped. Straightaway, Ben stood up.

'I'm healed! I'm healed!' Ben said, laughing and crying at the same time. He danced on the spot kicking his legs about.

'Look! Look! I can move!' he cried. 'God is so good!'

Everyone was astonished.

'Yes, God is good,' they agreed. 'What a fantastic thing to happen!'

The loaves and the fishes

JESUS and his special friends were so busy teaching and caring for the people, they got very tired.

'We all need to go away and have a rest,' said Jesus. 'Let's sail to the other side of the lake to be on our own.'

Jesus' friends were quite happy about this.

'I'm so tired,' yawned Andrew. 'I could fall asleep standing up.'

'When we reach the other side, you can have a long sleep,' said James.

But as they came close to the shore, they saw an enormous crowd of people. Something like five thousand people were waiting for them.

'Oh no!' groaned Philip, 'the people have followed us.'

'Tell us another story, Jesus,' the people called out.

Jesus smiled. 'These people are just like sheep who have lost their shepherd,' he thought.

But Jesus' friends weren't so understanding.

'I wish Jesus would send them all away,' grumbled James.

'Me too,' said Peter.

Instead, Jesus led everyone to a hillside where they all sat down to hear him speak. When it was growing dark, Jesus' friends came to him.

Philip said, 'It's past supper time and we're miles away from anywhere. Tell the people to go and get some food.'

'They don't need to go away,' replied Jesus. 'You can give them something to eat.'

Philip looked shocked. 'But we've got nothing to give them!' he complained.

'We've got a boy here with five loaves and two fishes but that's not enough to feed five thousand people,' grumbled Andrew.

'Tell the people to sit down in groups of about fifty,' Jesus said.

After they had done this, Jesus turned to the little boy.

'Here you are Jesus,' said the boy. 'It's all I've got but you can have it.'

Jesus smiled. 'Thank you,' he replied. Then taking the bread and fish he looked up to heaven and prayed:

'O Lord our God, King of the world, thank you for giving us all we need. Amen.'

Then Jesus put some of the food into the baskets which each of his twelve special friends carried with him.

'Now go and share this out,' said Jesus.

His friends looked at each other. They were very puzzled.

'If you say so,' they said.

The men began to walk around the groups, giving out the food. It took them ages. Each time they put a hand into their basket there was more food! The baskets just kept filling up! It was another miracle.

Jesus' friends were completely amazed. The people ate as much as they wanted. When they were all full up, Jesus said to his friends:

'Go and collect the leftovers. Let's not waste anything.'

So his friends walked around gathering the leftovers until they had twelve baskets full.

'How could Jesus do all this?' they puzzled. 'Where does he get this power from? What does it all mean?'

Jesus teaches the people

Many people believe that Jesus was the wisest teacher of all time.
When people gathered round to hear him, he sometimes told them stories
with a special lesson to help them understand God.

JESUS often taught people outside on the hills around Lake Galilee. There was plenty of room outdoors for lots of people to sit on the grass.

One day Jesus spent a long time talking about many different things. His special friends were there and lots of visitors who had come from all over the country to hear him teach. Jesus knew the people were poor but he had some good news for them.

'You think rich people are happier than you. It's not true. Poor people like you who trust in God are much happier than rich people.'

Jesus could see they were amazed.

'Most people think that being rich makes you happy,' the people murmured.

'Many rich people will never be happy because they think they don't need God.'

The people looked even more surprised when Jesus said this. Jesus gave them time to think, then he said:

'Because you love God, people may be unkind to you. But be happy about it. When you get to heaven you'll get a fantastic reward.'

'Good gracious! Jesus says some amazing things!' his friends thought. Everyone was quiet.

'Always be kind and generous,' Jesus told them, 'but don't give just so you can get something back.'

Some people squirmed.

'Jesus is right,' they thought. 'We don't like giving to people who can't give nice things back.'

Jesus' friends looked very thoughtful.

'Following Jesus isn't going to be easy,' they said to one another.

'If you do all I say you'll be like a wise man who built his house on hard rock,' said Jesus. 'The rain hammered down and the wind shook the walls and the flood waters rose higher and higher. But his house stayed up. It didn't fall down because it was built on rock.

But if you don't do what I say you'll be like the foolish man. He built his house on sand. When the rain hammered down and the wind shook the walls and the flood waters rose higher and higher, his house fell with a terrific crash!'

Everyone looked at each other. There was so much to think about. They all went home trying to remember all the things that Jesus had said. They had never heard anyone like him before. His special friends were amazed.

'When you listen to Jesus he makes all the laws that Moses gave us come to life. He talks as if he really knows what God thinks!' they said.

The good Samaritan

JESUS loved telling stories. Here is one he told to some teachers and lawyers.

One day a man was walking from Jericho down to Jerusalem. Suddenly, from behind some rocks, three angry-looking men appeared.

The man stopped and looked about. The road was empty. He gulped. 'Help, I'm all on my own,' he thought.

Next minute, the men pounced on him. Thump! Bash! Thump! Bash! They started to tear his clothes, to kick him and scratch his face.

'Help! Help!' yelled the man. But no-one came.

Thump! Bash! Thump! Bash!

The poor man fell on the ground. He was cut and bruised all over.

'Ow! Ow! Ow!' he moaned.

The three men just laughed and ran off.

Before long, the man heard some footsteps.

'There's someone coming,' he thought. He looked up and saw a priest.

'Help! Help!' he cried.

But as soon as the priest saw the man, he turned away and crossed over to the other side of the road.

'I'm keeping away,' the priest thought. 'I don't want to touch that man. He's half-dead anyway. I'm off.'

Some time later, the man heard more footsteps. He looked up. This time he saw a Jewish teacher.

'Help! Help!' the man groaned.

But as soon as the teacher saw the man, he also turned away and crossed over to the other side of the road.

'The robbers who attacked that man might still be around,' the teacher thought. 'I don't want any trouble. I'm off.'

Some time later, the man heard somebody else coming. He looked up again. This time he saw a Samaritan.

'Oh no! A Samaritan. He won't help me,' thought the man. 'He knows we Jews hate people from Samaria.'

But as soon as the Samaritan saw the man, he stopped.

'Oh dear, that poor man,' he thought. 'I must do something. He needs help.'

He slipped

down from his donkey and knelt beside the man.

'You'll be alright,' he said. 'I'll help you.'

He gently dabbed some cool wine and olive oil on the man's wounds to clean them and stop the pain. Then he covered his cuts with bandages.

'Thank you,' the man said weakly.

'I'm going to put you on my donkey,' the Samaritan explained, 'and take you somewhere safe.'

After lifting the man on to his donkey, the Samaritan led the donkey down the rocky path.

When they came to a small hotel, the Samaritan knocked at the door.

'I'd like a room for myself and this man,' he told the owner. That night the Samaritan stayed with the man and took care of him.

Next day, he said to the hotel owner:

'Here is some money. Look after this man until I return.' He handed the owner enough money to pay for a two-week stay. 'If you need any more money,' he said, 'I will pay you later.'

The hotel owner agreed and the Samaritan went on his way.

'Now,' asked Jesus, 'which of these men acted like a neighbour to the man who had been beaten up?'

'The one who was kind to him,' replied a lawyer.

'Go then and love your neighbour like this,' said Jesus.

The lost son

J ESUS told people many stories to help them understand his teaching. Here is one of them.

There was once a man who had two sons. The father had promised them some money.

'It's not fair having to wait,' the younger son muttered. 'I need that money now! I'm not waiting any longer.' He stormed out of the house, stamping his feet.

'Father! Father!' he shouted loudly.

'Yes, son,' replied his father.

'I want my share of the money now!'

'If that's what you really want, then you may have it,' his father answered kindly.

The youngest son was delighted. Within a few days he had left home with his fortune and was spending it as fast as he could. He gave lots of big parties and bought wonderful presents and food and drink for all his new friends.

But soon all the money had gone and so had his friends. The only job he could find was looking after some pigs. As he watched the pigs guzzling out of the trough, his stomach rumbled.

'I'm so hungry,' he thought. 'I could eat out of the trough myself.'

He thought about his home and family.

'I've been so stupid, wasting all that money. I'll go home and say I'm sorry. Perhaps Father will forgive me and give me a job.'

Several days later, just as he approached the house, his heart was thumping loudly.

'I hope Father *will* forgive me,' he thought.

Meanwhile, his father had been hoping his son would return.

When he saw his son walking up the path, he dashed out and ran towards him. With a great bear hug, he swept his son off his feet and kissed him.

'Father, I'm sorry, I've behaved so badly,' the boy said. 'I don't deserve to be called your son anymore.'

His father didn't seem to hear a word.

'Servants!' he called. 'Bring out the best clothes and put them on my son. Prepare the best food in the house. We're going to have a big party. My son, who I thought was lost, is home again!'

Now the older son was out working in the fields. When he returned to the house he heard music and dancing.

'What's going on?' he asked one of the servants.

'Your brother has come home,' the man replied.

The older brother was furious.

'It's not fair!' he shouted loudly at his father. 'I've always done as I was told. But you never gave *me* a party. How can you be so nice to *him* when he's wasted all that money?'

'My son,' his father said gently, 'try not to be jealous. I know you've never left me and everything I have belongs to you. Your brother left us but now he is back home so we must be happy. He was lost but now he is found.'

Zaccheus listens to Jesus

*After they had met Jesus, many people's lives were completely changed.
I'm sure Zaccheus, who climbed a tree to see Jesus, would never have guessed
what a difference Jesus was going to make to him.*

ONE day, Jesus was talking to a large crowd of people. Zaccheus was trying to push his way to the front of the crowd so he could see Jesus.

'Please let me through,' he pleaded. 'I'm only small.'

'We're not letting you in,' said the crowd. 'Go away, you little pest!'

Nobody liked Zaccheus because he made people pay taxes and he always kept some money for himself. That way, he became very rich.

'I know! I'll climb to the top of a tree,' thought Zaccheus.

When he got to the top he could see everything and Jesus could see him.

'Come down, Zaccheus,' Jesus called. 'I am coming to your house for a meal.'

Zaccheus was so surprised he nearly fell out of the tree. He scrambled down and landed at Jesus' feet.

'That makes me so happy,' said Zaccheus, jumping for joy.

The crowd were shocked!

'Jesus is going to Zaccheus' house,' they said. 'Surely Jesus must know he's a thief.'

Zaccheus was so pleased Jesus had picked him out. For the first time in his life, he felt very special.

'I am not going to steal any more,' he thought. 'Jesus loves me and that matters more than anything in the whole wide world.'

He decided to make a speech.

'From now on I will give half of all I own to the poor. If I have cheated anybody I will pay them back four times what I took.'

The crowd gasped, Zaccheus was saying sorry!

Jesus smiled. 'Zaccheus, you have done more than you needed to,' he said. 'Now you belong to God's family. This is why God sent me. To help people like you who are lost.'

Jesus enters Jerusalem

WHEN people saw and heard what Jesus did, many of them began to trust and follow him. But some others wanted to make trouble. They went to the Pharisees, the strict Jewish teachers, and told them what Jesus was doing.

'We don't like it either,' grumbled the Pharisees. 'The people have stopped listening to us ever since Jesus came along. We must try and get rid of him.'

So the Pharisees gave this order:

'If anyone knows where Jesus is, they must tell us so we can arrest him.'

Now Jesus was on his way to Jerusalem. It was the Passover festival and there were crowds of excited people all around. When he came close to the city, he sent two of his friends on a special errand.

'Go to the nearest village,' he said. 'When you arrive, you will find a donkey tied up. No-one has ever ridden him. Untie the donkey and bring him to me. If anyone asks, "Why are you untying the donkey?" say, "The Lord needs it."'

So his friends did as Jesus asked. They found the donkey and, as they were untying it, the owner rushed over and said, 'Oi! That's my donkey! Why are you untying him?'

Jesus' friends replied, 'The Lord needs it.'

Immediately the owner knew the donkey was for Jesus so he let them take it.

Clip, clop, clip, clop! went the hoofs of the donkey as they walked back down the cobbled road to where Jesus was waiting.

Jesus' friends threw their coats on the donkey's back to make a saddle. Then they helped Jesus to get on.

Clip, clop! Clip, clop! As the donkey carried Jesus towards Jerusalem, crowds of people spread out their coats and put down palm branches on the ground for the donkey to walk over.

The crowd began to shout:

'Jesus is King! Long live the King! God bless the King! Praise God!'

Everyone was really excited except for the Pharisees. They were furious. Jesus' friends became very worried.

'Jesus, tell the people to be quiet. Can't you hear what they are saying about you?' they shouted.

But Jesus replied, 'It's impossible to stop them'.

The Pharisees scowled. 'He'll be sorry,' they thought. 'We won't let him get away with this. Things are getting worse. More and more people are following Jesus. We must put a stop to it before he has more power than we do.'

Jesus is angry in the temple

Can you imagine what sort of person Jesus was?
We know he was loving and forgiving, but he sometimes became angry
when people were dishonest and forgot about God.

A S soon as Jesus reached Jerusalem he went straight to the Jewish temple. It was a beautiful building. There were huge creamy-coloured stone walls, smooth shiny marble columns and glittering gold decorations. But Jesus was not pleased with what he saw.

The temple had been built so people could come for prayer and to learn more about God. But the people weren't praying at all. They were busy buying and selling.

'Come and buy my lovely doves. Save money if you buy two!'

'This way, ladies and gentlemen, for sheep and goats. Only the best!'

'Honest John, that's my name. The best prices in town.'

Jesus was furious. He could also see these men were charging far too much for their goods so they could make themselves lots of money.

'It's no use telling the priests,' thought Jesus. 'They won't do anything. I'll have to do it myself.'

Jesus looked around and saw some rope. He quickly tied some knots in it until it looked like a whip. Crack! Jesus whacked the rope on the ground. Everyone looked up, startled.

Who was this man? What was he doing?

Crack! Crack! Animals began to run about. 'Baa! Baa!' bleated the lambs. 'Neh! Neh!' went the goats.

Crack! Crack! Jesus herded the animals towards the temple doors.

'Oi! Leave those animals alone!' shouted the traders.

But it was too late. The animals were escaping and running free outside.

Then Jesus strode up to the tables where great piles of coins were stacked high. He turned the tables upside down, spilling the coins on to the ground so they rolled all over the place.

The moneychangers couldn't decide whether to shout at Jesus or to run after their precious coins.

But Jesus wasn't frightened of them. He shouted at them:

'How dare you do this to my Father's house! You have turned God's house into a market-place for cheats!'

The priests, who had been watching all this, didn't dare say anything. They knew the traders were doing wrong. But they were still very angry with Jesus.

'Show us a miracle to prove you have a right to cause all this fuss!' they ordered.

Jesus pointed to himself.

'Tear this temple down and in three days I will build it again,' he said.

'He must be stupid,' the priests thought.

'It took forty-six years to build this temple,' they laughed, 'so how could you possibly build it again in three days!'

But Jesus wasn't really talking about the building. He was talking about himself. In a few days time they would find out what he really meant.

Jesus' last night

The next stories are about what happened to Jesus at a time we now call Easter.
Part of the story is very sad, but the ending is wonderful. When you believe in Jesus,
you believe that these are the most important events that have ever happened.

AFTER Jesus had thrown everyone out of the temple, the chief priests were even more determined to arrest him.

'We can't arrest him in front of the crowds,' they agreed. 'They might make trouble. We must do it when no-one is around.'

Their chance came when one of Jesus' friends, Judas, came to them.

'What will you give me if I tell you where you can find Jesus on his own?' Judas asked.

'You can have thirty pieces of silver,' the priests said, delighted.

Judas nodded. 'You'll hear from me soon,' he replied.

The day came for the Passover meal when all Jewish people remember the time God rescued them from slavery in Egypt.

Jesus told Peter and John to go to Jerusalem.

'You'll meet a man carrying a jar of water,' Jesus told them. 'Follow him into the house he enters. Tell the man who owns the house, "The teacher is coming here to eat the Passover."'

So Peter and John found the house and spoke to the owner.

'The teacher is coming here to eat the Passover,' they said.

As soon as the owner heard this, he knew they meant Jesus, and agreed to give them a room.

That evening, Jesus and his twelve special friends met at the house to eat the Passover. It was a celebration meal but Jesus seemed strangely sad. As they were eating, Jesus picked up the bread. He began to break it into small pieces and share it around.

'Eat this,' said Jesus, 'and remember I gave my life for you.'

Then Jesus took a cup of wine.

'Drink this,' said Jesus, 'and remember I came to forgive many people.'

Jesus' friends looked at one another.

'What does Jesus mean?' they wondered.

'One of you is going to turn against me,' Jesus went on.

His friends were even more puzzled. Who could it be? Suddenly Judas got up from the table.

'Be quick,' Jesus said to him. Judas turned and left.

'Perhaps Jesus has given Judas a job to do,' the others thought. It was all very strange. They could not understand what was going on.

Much later that night, after the meal, Jesus and his friends went to a quiet place, the Garden of Gethsemane.

'You will all let me down,' Jesus said quietly.

'I'll never do that!' said Peter loudly.

'Peter, you will pretend that you don't even know me. You will do this three times then the cock will crow,' said Jesus.

Peter looked shocked.

'Now I must pray alone,' said Jesus. 'Stay here and wait for me.'

His friends were tired and fell asleep. When Jesus came back he said:

'Why are you sleeping? Get up and see who is coming.'

Suddenly Judas appeared, followed by some Roman soldiers and a crowd, carrying sticks and swords. Judas came up to Jesus and kissed him on the cheek, then two soldiers stepped forward and grabbed Jesus by the arms.

His friends watched in horror as they took Jesus away.

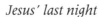

Only Peter felt brave enough to follow behind as the soldiers led Jesus to the chief priest's house. Peter waited outside. A young maid saw him and said:

'You were with Jesus.'

'Not me,' said Peter, 'I don't know him.'

A little later a man stared at Peter then said:

'You were with Jesus.'

'Oh no, I wasn't!' Peter answered.

An hour later another man passed him and said:

'I'm sure you were with Jesus.'

'I don't know what you're talking about,' said Peter crossly.

Then a cock crowed. 'Cock-a-doodle-doo!' Peter remembered that Jesus had said this would happen. He was terribly upset and walked away, sobbing.

Jesus dies on the cross

THE soldiers who were guarding Jesus tied a blindfold over his eyes. Slap! One man hit him hard, then another.

'Guess who hit you,' they laughed.

Then they took Jesus to the chief priests who asked him lots of questions.

'Are you the Son of God?' they asked.

'You say that I am,' replied Jesus.

The priests looked pleased.

'He could have said no, but he didn't,' they said to each other.

'That means he does think he's the Son of God.'

'You deserve death for saying that,' they told Jesus.

Because only the Romans had the power to put a man to death, the priests took Jesus to the Roman ruler, Pontius Pilate.

'This man says he is a king,' they told him.

'Are you the King of the Jews?' Pilate asked.

'You say that I am,' Jesus replied.

'But that isn't bad enough for me to have him killed,' Pilate told the priests.

'But he's a troublemaker,' complained the priests. 'He's been a troublemaker ever since he left Galilee.'

'Ahh!' said Pilate. 'If he comes from Galilee you must take him to Herod. He's in charge of Galilee.'

When Herod met Jesus, he asked him lots of questions. He was hoping Jesus would perform a miracle. But Jesus said nothing. Herod grew bored.

'Send him back to Pilate!' he ordered angrily. So they returned to Pilate.

Pilate called together all the chief priests, the Pharisees and other people.

'This man Jesus has done nothing wrong,' Pilate told them. 'I'll have him whipped, then set free.'

'No!' cried the crowd. 'Kill him and let Barabbas go free!' Barabbas was in prison for murder.

'But Jesus has done nothing wrong!' Pilate repeated.

'Kill him! Put him on the cross!' the crowd yelled.

'I will have him whipped, then let him go!' said Pilate.

'No! No! Kill him!' the crowd yelled more loudly.

By this time Pilate was very worried. Finally he gave in.

'I sentence Jesus to death on a cross,' he said. 'Set Barabbas free!'

'Hurrah!' cried the crowd.

The soldiers took Jesus, ripped off his shirt and beat his bare back with a whip. Then they put a crown made from spiky thorns on his head and a purple cloak on his back.

'You don't look like a king to us!' they laughed cruelly.

They hit him again. Then they pulled off the cloak and put his shirt back on.

The soldiers made Jesus walk, carrying his cross, to the place outside Jerusalem where he would be crucified. When he stumbled, exhausted, they gave the great wooden cross to a man called Simon to carry.

Thud! Bang! A soldier hammered nails into Jesus' feet and hands so he was fixed to the cross. Then they lifted the cross up and pushed it into the ground.

Two other men, both criminals, were also nailed on crosses on each side of Jesus.

Jesus cried out, 'Father, forgive them because they don't know what they are doing.'

The crowds watched. It grew dark.

Suddenly Jesus called out, 'My God, my God, why have you left me?'

Then he died.

Jesus lives again

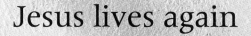

AFTER he died, Jesus' body still hung on the cross. A Jewish leader called Joseph went to see Pilate.

'Please can I have the body of Jesus?' he asked bravely.

Pilate agreed, so Joseph took Jesus' body down. With his friend, Nicodemus, he wrapped the body in a clean cloth and placed it in his own tomb, a large cave cut out of the rock. Then they rolled a great stone across the opening of the tomb.

Next day, being Saturday, no-one visited the tomb as it was the day when all Jewish people rested.

The day after, Mary Magdalene and other women who followed Jesus went to the tomb. They were taking perfume to put on Jesus' body so it would smell sweetly.

Walking up to the tomb, Mary asked:

'Who will help us move the stone away?' Then she gasped. The stone had already been rolled away!

The women looked inside the tomb. It was empty!

'Where's Jesus?' they cried.

Suddenly an angel appeared. The women trembled. They had never seen an angel before!

'Don't be afraid,' the angel said. 'I know you are looking for Jesus. He isn't here. But you will see him again. He has come back from death.'

Then the angel disappeared.

'Jesus is alive!' cried Mary. 'We must tell the others.' The women raced to tell Jesus' friends.

'Jesus is alive! He's not dead any more,' they cried excitedly.

'Don't talk nonsense,' Jesus' friends said crossly. 'We know he's dead.'

Later that day, Jesus' friends met together. Everyone was worried.

'Lock the doors,' said John. 'They've killed Jesus. It could be us next.'

Suddenly Jesus himself stood there.

'Peace be with you,' said Jesus.

'It's a g- g- ghost!' stuttered James.

'Don't be scared,' said Jesus. 'Why can't you believe it's really me? Touch me. Ghosts don't have skin and bones.'

That evening Jesus stayed with them to talk about his life, his death and the future.

Next morning they told Thomas what had happened.

'Thomas, we've seen Jesus! Isn't it fantastic?' they cried.

'I'll only believe you if I see him myself,' said Thomas.

A week passed. Jesus' friends met together again. Suddenly Jesus appeared. Thomas stared and stared.

'Come here, Thomas,' said Jesus. 'Touch my hands and believe.'

Thomas walked up close to Jesus and touched his hands. He could feel the scars where the nails had been.

It was true! Jesus was alive! Thomas fell on his knees.

'My Lord and my God!' he cried.

'You believe because you have seen me,' said Jesus. 'How happy people will be who have never seen me, but still believe.'

During the next forty days Jesus appeared to people in all kinds of places.

One day Peter said, 'I'm fed up doing nothing. I'm going fishing.'

Six friends decided to go with him and they set sail. They fished all night but caught nothing. As they sailed back to shore a man appeared.

'Have you caught anything?' he called out.

'Nothing,' they answered. 'Not even a tiddler.'

'Throw your nets over the side,' he said firmly.

'Ok, let's try,' said Peter.

They threw the nets out. Flip, flap, flip! The nets filled up with fish!

Peter looked at the man again. 'It's Jesus!' he shouted.

When they landed the boat, Jesus was cooking some fish over a fire.

'Come and eat,' said Jesus.

No-one dared say, 'Who are you?'

They all knew, it was Jesus.

Jesus goes to heaven

WHEN Jesus died on the cross his special friends were very sad, frightened and worried. But when he began appearing to them again they became very excited.

'It's almost too good to be true,' they said. 'It's the most amazing thing that has ever happened.'

Whenever Jesus appeared he also taught them new things.

'Go round the world and tell everyone this good news. I forgive all who believe in me and follow me. But don't leave Jerusalem yet. Wait until God gives you the gift of the Holy Spirit.'

'What's the Holy Spirit?' His friends were puzzled.

Time passed. Then one day when the friends met together on a mountain outside Jerusalem called the Mount of Olives, Jesus appeared again.

They did not know this would be the last time they would see him on earth.

They asked him, 'Are you going to free Israel from the Roman rulers?'

'Only God knows these things,' replied Jesus. 'It is God's secret. But when the Holy Spirit comes, you will have the power to become my messengers in Jerusalem, Judea, Samaria and all over the world.'

When Jesus had finished speaking his friends watched in wonder as he began to rise into the sky and disappeared into a heavenly cloud.

'Is he coming back? Where's he gone?' they asked, staring up into the sky.

Suddenly there were two angels standing beside them.

'Men of Galilee, why are you standing here looking up? Jesus has gone to heaven and one day he will come back in the same kind of way.'

The angels disappeared. Jesus' friends looked at one another. First, Jesus had died. Then he had come back to life. Now he had gone to heaven. Whatever was going to happen next?

God sends his Holy Spirit

When Jesus left the earth, his followers were very worried and upset.
How could so few people carry on Jesus' work? Here's how they discovered
God wasn't going to leave them on their own.

TEN days after Jesus rose up to heaven, his friends held a meeting for about one hundred and twenty people, all of whom believed Jesus had come back to life. It was the Day of Pentecost, when Jewish people thanked God for harvest-time.

As the crowd chatted, there came a noise which sounded like the wind. Then they saw what looked like flames of fire over the head of each person. Everyone was filled with God's Holy Spirit and had the power to talk in a completely new language. The noise they made was incredibly beautiful.

Now there were hundreds of Jewish visitors in Jerusalem. They had come from many different countries to enjoy the festival. When they heard the noise, they rushed over.

'What's going on?' they asked excitedly. 'Listen to those people! We have come from many different countries but it sounds like they know how to speak our languages. What does it mean?'

But there were other people who just made fun of Jesus' followers.

'They've been drinking too much wine,' they laughed.

When Peter heard that, he stood up and spoke in a loud voice.

'Listen everybody! We are not drunk. It's too early in the morning to be drinking wine. No! What you see was written many years ago. God said he would send the Holy Spirit on everyone, not just special people like Moses and Elijah. God said there would be miracles and fantastic things would happen. And whoever turned to Jesus would be forgiven.'

Peter went on, 'Jesus came to us and proved that God had sent him. He taught, he healed, he loved us. Then you killed him on the cross. But God brought him back to life because death has no power over Jesus. Now Jesus is giving us God's Holy Spirit!'

When the crowd heard this, they were confused.

'What shall we do?' they asked.

'Each one of you must be sorry for all the things you have done wrong and believe in Jesus,' Peter replied. 'Be baptised and ask God to give you his Holy Spirit. He will clean you from the inside and give you the power to be God's messengers.'

Many who were listening believed what Peter said.

'We believe God has forgiven us,' they said. 'We want to be baptised today!'

And that day about three thousand people were baptised.

The new believers stayed to learn more from Jesus' friends, to pray and to share bread and wine together just as Jesus had taught them. They met in the temple to pray and praise God, and every day more and more people believed in Jesus.

Peter escapes from prison

*People who believe in Jesus are called Christians. In the early days,
their job of telling other people about Jesus was very difficult and dangerous.*

ONE afternoon, Peter and John went to the temple to pray. On their way they saw a man being carried to the temple gates. When they reached the gate, the man called out:

'Spare a few coins. I've not walked since the day I was born.' He held out his hands and bowed his head.

'Look at us,' Peter said.

The man lifted his head, hoping they would give him some money.

But Peter said, 'I have no money but I give you what I have. In the name of Jesus I tell you to get up and walk!'

Peter took hold of the man's right hand and began to help him up.

At once the man's feet and ankles became strong. He jumped up and began to walk.

'I can walk!' he cried. He was so happy he began to dance.

'Thank you, God!' he sang, and clapped his hands for joy.

When the people saw him they were amazed.

'Isn't this the man who sits begging at the temple?' they asked.

'It can't be the same person, can it?'

But it was. The man went into the temple with Peter and John, laughing and leaping because of what God had done for him.

Inside the temple, Peter taught anyone who wanted to hear about Jesus. Day after day, crowds of people came to listen. Peter and his friends healed other sick people, too, and the news of Jesus coming back to life spread all through Jerusalem.

When the Pharisees heard about what was happening they were extremely jealous. To please the Pharisees, Herod Agrippa, the new king, decided that Peter ought to be arrested.

'Throw this Peter

into prison,' he ordered. 'Guards! Don't let him escape. He must be killed.'

Day after day, Peter's friends prayed:

'Please God, keep Peter safe. Bring him out of prison.'

The night before Herod planned to put Peter to death, Peter was fast asleep. He was handcuffed to two guards and outside the prison door stood another two guards.

Suddenly, an angel appeared. He shook Peter gently and whispered:

'Wake up, Peter! Get up! Hurry!'

Peter stood up clumsily, half-asleep. His handcuffs slipped off and fell to the floor.

'Put on your sandals and cloak,' said the angel, 'and follow me.'

Peter followed, completely bewildered.

'Is this real? Or am I dreaming?' he muttered to himself in amazement.

They walked past the sleeping guards, through the prison doors, and out into the dark street. Once outside, the angel vanished.

'I'm free!' Peter gasped. 'It's not a dream after all.'

He raced to find his friends. 'They'll be at Mary's house,' he guessed.

He was right. Inside the house he could hear his friends praying. Peter knocked at the door.

A maid called out, 'Who's there?'

'It's Peter,' he whispered.

The maid was astounded! She ran back into the room to Peter's friends.

'Peter is here!' she cried.

'Don't be so silly!' everyone said.

Meanwhile Peter kept knocking. At last they opened the door.

'Peter!' they gasped, 'It's true!'

'God sent an angel to rescue me,' Peter explained. 'But I can't stay here. I must go before the guards come looking for me.'

So Peter left and went to a secret place to hide. Next morning, when the guards woke up they couldn't believe their eyes.

'The prisoner's escaped! However did he get out?' they gasped.

When Herod heard the news he was furious.

'My plan is ruined!' he yelled. 'Now Peter is free to tell more and more people about Jesus!'

Paul turns to God

PETER, John and many other followers of Jesus went all over Jerusalem telling people the fantastic news that Jesus had come back to life.

Now the Pharisees and chief priests were hoping people would forget about Jesus. They were disappointed. More and more people believed in him and began to meet together to share their faith.

One day the Pharisees arrested a believer, called Stephen, for talking about Jesus. Stephen told them:

'You are God's enemies. Jesus will judge you for what you have done. He is waiting to welcome me into heaven.'

When the Pharisees and priests heard this they were furious. They picked up stones and hurled them at Stephen until he was dead.

A Pharisee called Paul stood and watched.

'That man deserved to die,' he thought, 'and so do all the other believers. I shall kill them myself!'

From then on, Paul ordered many believers, men and women, to be thrown into prison. Hundreds of other believers ran away to different towns, frightened that they, too, would be caught and punished.

But Paul followed them. He went first to the city of Damascus.

'If I find any believers here, I'll capture them,' he said.

But on his way to Damascus something amazing happened! A brilliant, dazzling white light flashed around him.

Paul fell on his knees. 'I can't see!' he cried out.

A voice called out, 'Why are you hurting me?'

'Who are you?' Paul asked.

'I am Jesus, whom you are hurting,' the voice said. 'Get up and go to Damascus where you will be told what to do.'

Paul stood up slowly. He opened his eyes.

'I'm blind!' he cried.

Paul's friends didn't know what to think.

'Hold on to me,' one of them said. 'I'll lead you to Damascus.'

For the next three days Paul stayed blind and was too shocked to eat or drink.

Meanwhile, God spoke to a believer in Damascus called Ananias.

'Go to Straight Street and ask for a man called Paul. He is praying. I have told him you will come and take his blindness away.'

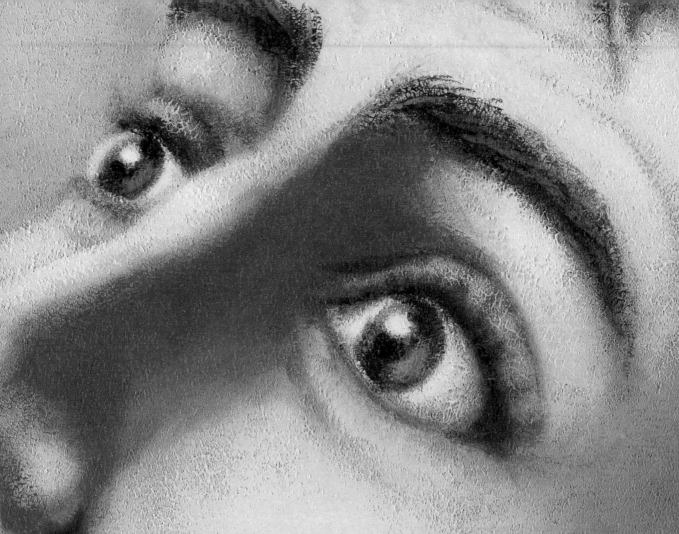

'But God,' replied Ananias, 'he might kill me! Everyone knows Paul is trying to have all the believers killed.'

'Go!' said God. 'I have chosen Paul to be my messenger.'

So Ananias obeyed God. When he found Paul he prayed:

'Brother Paul, God has sent me so you may see again and be filled with his Holy Spirit.'

Paul opened his eyes. 'I *can* see again!' he cried.

'God has chosen you to be his messenger,' said Ananias. 'Be baptised and remember God has forgiven you.'

For the next few days Paul stayed in Damascus. Then he started to go out and talk about Jesus to anyone who would listen.

Everyone was astonished.

'We thought Paul was trying to kill the believers. What's going on? Has he really changed? Will it last?' they wondered.

But Paul kept on talking about Jesus whatever happened. Sometimes he was put in prison. Sometimes he was exhausted and sad. But he carried on. For many years he travelled to different countries spreading the good news about Jesus. He never forgot what happened to him that day on the road to Damascus.

Epilogue

Just think – if it hadn't been for brave men like Peter and Paul, who lived nearly 2,000 years ago, and who were treated very badly because they believed in Jesus, there might be no-one around today who could pass on the Christian story. Instead, there are now millions of men and women and boys and girls, in countries all over the world, who believe it's very important to tell other people the good news about Jesus.

In our prayers to God, it would be good to thank him for the different people we've read about in these Bible stories, but perhaps we should thank him most of all for sending Jesus to be our friend and to show us what is good.